Programming Techniques
for
Object-Based
Statistical Analysis
with
SAS® Software

Tanya Kolosova
Samuel Berestizhevsky

Comments or Questions?

The author assumes complete responsibility for the technical accuracy of the content of this book. If you have any questions about the material in this book, please write to the author at this address:

> SAS Institute Inc.
> Books by Users
> Attn: Tanya Kolosava and Samuel Berestizhevsky
> SAS Campus Drive
> Cary, NC 27513

If you prefer, you can send e-mail to sasbbu@sas.com with "comments for Tanya Kolosava and Samuel Berestizhevsky" as the subject line, or you can fax the Books by Users program at (919) 677-4444.

The correct bibliographic citation for this manual is as follows: Tanya Kolosava and Samuel Berestizhevsky, *Programming Techniques for Object-Based Software Analysis with SAS® Software*, Cary, NC: SAS Institute Inc., 1998. 152 pp.

Programming Techniques for Object-Based Software Analysis with SAS® Software

Copyright © 1998 by SAS Institute Inc., Cary, NC, USA.

ISBN 1-58025-198-6

Table of Contents

Preface

Object-oriented programming is a style of software development that models the relationships among the objects that comprise a problem rather than procedures which can be taken to solve the problem. Objects may model both data and actions (operations) that can logically be maintained together.

Moving to object-oriented statistical programming and analysis requires a shift in thinking away from the procedural model – where data is passed into a procedural hierarchy – to a new model where procedure execution is a result of relationships among objects. This new model is more declarative, meaning that objects are first declared then allowed to act or interact. This manner of actions makes it easier to design and implement statistical analyses, which take the actions they do only as reaction to object state.

Goals of the book

The goals of this book are

- to provide an understanding of concepts of object-oriented statistical programming and analysis.

- to demonstrate SAS software's ability to implement an object-oriented approach to statistical programming and analysis.

You, the reader

This book is for data analysts, statisticians, and SAS programmers.

We consider the data analyst an end-user of statistical classes, one who performs data and statistical analysis but who does not necessarily know programming with the SAS System. Further in the book you will see that the data analyst operates with statistical classes in a specially created table-driven environment, and needs only to be acquainted with its very simple interface. The statistician is the designer of new statistical classes and their actions. We assume the statistician is familiar with SAS software's capabilities for analyzing data. The SAS programmer is the person who develops programs implementing object-oriented statistical programming and analysis. This person should have at least average skills with the SAS System.

Our goal is to incorporate new classes of objects into SAS applications in a seamless way, without any explicit action on the end-user's part. At the same time, we wish to simplify the job of the statisticians in designing new classes of objects. Data analysts will continue to see only the action, so their view of the SAS macro language will not be affected. And finally, the notion of inheritance – that new classes can automatically inherit actions written for existing classes – reduces the amount of programming for programmers.

The object-oriented approach to statistical analysis and programming enables the data analyst, statistician, and programmer to operate as an effective team for solving data analysis problems. In turn, the process of problem solving becomes much more structured and documented.

First, the data analyst structures data and defines a data object in the tables of the data dictionary. Then this data object is associated with an appropriate statistical class. The data analyst uses the actions of this statistical class to perform data analysis.

The statistical classes are designed by the statistician. Statistical knowledge, combined with understanding of a specific problem, enables the statistician to generalize the problem and create a class that is suitable for a specific group of problems. Each time a new problem arises that does not yet have an appropriate class, the statistician creates one.

Once the programs supporting the object-oriented approach are developed, the programmer has only to implement methods for new classes, often re-using previously written code.

How to use this book

This book examines various issues that are related to the design, development and implementation of an object-oriented approach to statistical programming and analysis in SAS. To get the most from this book, we suggest you read the chapters in order.

The complete source codes for the programming examples in this book, as well as extra programs, are available from SAS Institute through the SAS Online Samples facility (for detailed information, refer to the inside back cover of this book).

Organization

This book is divided into five chapters. Most of the chapters have a very similar structure: an introduction that highlights its main subjects, a full discussion of those objects, and a summary that acts as a transition to succeeding chapters. Each chapter demonstrates concepts through examples that are placed in separate sections for the statistician, the data analyst, and the programmer.

Chapter 1. Introduction to Object-Oriented Statistical Programming introduces the principles of object-oriented statistical programming and analysis, and defines the main terms that are used in the book.

Chapter 2. Statistical Objects explains the process of defining statistical classes such as Vector, Discrete Vector, Matrix, and Data Table, along with their attributes and some of their actions.

Chapter 3. Statistical Programming explains how to create a set of actions that specify how a statistical object will behave with respect to certain generic actions. This chapter provides reusable SAS macro programs for performing generic statistical actions in SAS.

Chapter 4. Data Dictionary for Classes and Methods Definitions focuses on the design of the table-driven environment for object-oriented statistical data analysis in SAS. This chapter shows how to define statistical actions for specific types of data objects, and shows how to write reusable SAS macro programs to implement actions.

Chapter 5. Example: Object-Oriented Time Series Analysis shows how to create, visualize, and process time series in SAS using an object-oriented approach to statistical programming and analysis.

Conventions

In this book, you will see several type styles used to present text, syntax, and special structures. Style conventions are summarized here:

plain	the basic type style used for most text.
Mixed Case	used for table names and action parameters.
UPPERCASE	used for data elements (columns) and format names. Uppercase is also used for SAS statements and other SAS language elements when they appear in the text.
Italic	used for class names (with initial caps) and to show emphasis.
bold	used for object names.
`monospace`	used to show examples of programming code, macro code, and for parameter names when they appear in text.
`_method()`	represents a class method name.

Acknowledgments

This book is dedicated to our beloved children, Hannah, Noah, Yoav, and Asnat.

It is the result of many years of developing statistical applications and working with our customers. We would especially like to thank the research staff of Intel Development Center in Haifa, Israel, and the statistical process control staff of Tower Semiconductor in Migdal-Ha'Emek, Israel, who tested and commented on our approach to object-oriented statistical programming and analysis with SAS.

We would like to thank Julie Platt, our editor at SAS Institute, Sue Kocher, our copyeditor, Aaron Bittner, and other members of the editorial staff for their support and assistance in preparing this book for publication.

We would also like to thank Samuel's parents, Joseph and Raya, and our neighbors Abraham and Zippora Amado who supported a creative atmosphere while we were writing the book.

CHAPTER 1

Introduction to Object-Oriented Statistical Programming

Introduction

An object-oriented approach to statistical programming and analysis focuses attention on the content of the statistical model, but not on the details of the computation. This programming and analysis style enables you to perform analyses using only statistical categories, while making computations transparent. Such a style is implemented through the use of classes and the relationships between them.

Here are definitions for the main terms that we use in the book:

class	the template or model for a statistical object, which includes data describing the object's characteristics (attributes) and actions that it can perform.
attribute	a characteristic associated with a statistical object. All objects of the same class have the same set of attributes. These attributes are specified by name, type, and initial value, and they are automatically initialized when an object is created.
action	an operation that is defined for a class and can be executed by any object created from that class.

A specific representation of a class is called an object, and a specific implementation of an action for a specific class is called a method. An object inherits all the attributes of its class as well as the actions that the class can execute.

In this book we consider only three kinds of relationships between classes: inheritance, superclass/subclass, and abstract superclass. Inheritance is the mechanism that allows class *One* to inherit the attributes and actions of class *Two* without the need to recreate/redefine them. The class *One* should supply only attributes and actions that need to be different from those inherited. If class *One* inherits from class *Two*, then *Two* is called superclass of *One*, and *One* is called subclass of *Two*. With inheritance, we enable a subclass to offer the same properties as their superclasses. Class *Two* can be an abstract superclass if it is only used as a superclass for other classes. In this case, class *Two* only specifies attributes, and its subclasses must define the attributes of *Two*.

To highlight the differences between a class and an object, and between an action and a method, we use special style conventions (see "Conventions" in the Preface). For example: "The **vector** object of the *Vector Discrete* class uses the _dcreate() method that implements the Create action.

We have implemented the object-oriented approach to statistical programming and analysis using the previously developed table-driven environment described in our earlier book[1]. The table-driven environment provides you with a convenient and reliable environment for statistical object-oriented programming and analysis. The table-driven environment contains the data dictionary and its supporting programs. At the heart of this environment is the set of specially structured tables that form the data dictionary. The data dictionary contains information concerning classes, their attributes, and actions (Chapter 4 describes the data dictionary in detail). The SAS System with our table-driven environment allows you to define classes of objects. Using this environment, you can easily and quickly extend the set of already-created classes.

In this chapter, we guide you through several simple examples that show how to implement a mechanism of object-oriented statistical programming and analysis with the SAS System. The use of the actions allows programming in SAS to have much more of the style of object-oriented programming systems. However, because we use the table-driven environment, methods that implement actions are not restricted to automatic invocation, and they can be used like any other SAS macro function.

Fundamentals of Object-Oriented Programming

In object-oriented programming, you consider a class of objects and try to imagine all the actions you may want to perform on such objects. You then define data attributes and actions specifically for that class of objects.

In this book, the type of object will be specified only when it is necessary to distinguish between them, or when the type of object is not clear from the context. Otherwise, 'object' refers to both data and statistical objects.

For example, suppose you want to create an array of numbers as a statistical object, and you want to print the data contained in that object. Using the object-oriented approach to statistical analysis, you can define a class of objects called *Vector*, and then define actions for generating an object of this class and printing data that is contained by this object. These two actions, just as an example, can be defined for a wide variety of classes, but might need to be implemented differently for each of them.

An action that is common to a wide variety of classes is called a generic action. The actual implementation of an action for a specific class is called a method. Actions are carried out by means of a mechanism that identifies the class of arguments and calls the appropriate methods.

The definition of a new class is performed in the tables of the data dictionary. The data dictionary is a set of tables with strictly defined relations that stores definitions of classes, methods, objects, and so on. (Chapter 4 describes the data dictionary in detail.) Each class, its attributes, and its methods should be defined in three tables: Class, ClassAtr, and ClassMet. In Chapter 2 we will discuss in detail how to define a new class

---

[1] Kolosava, Tanya and Berestizhevsky, Samuel, *Table-Driven Strategies for Rapid SAS Applications Development*, Cary, NC: SAS Institute, Inc., 1995

in the data dictionary, but here is a very simple example of a definition of the *Vector* and *Vector Discrete* classes. The Class table defines and describes the classes:

Class Table

CLASS	SPRCLASS	Description
Vector	Main	Array of continuous numbers
Vector Discrete	Vector	Array of discrete numbers

These two rows in the Class table define the following:

- There is a *Vector* class that specifies attributes and actions on an array of continuous numbers. This class is a subclass of the *Main* class (an abstract superclass that will be defined in Chapter 2).

- There is a *Vector Discrete* class that specifies attributes and actions on an array of discrete numbers, and it is derived from the *Vector* class.

The ClassAtr table contains a definition of class attributes for each class:

ClassAtr table

CLASS	ATTR_NO	ATTRNAME	ATTRDESC
Vector	1	OBJECT	Name of the data object producing an object of the Vector class.
Vector	2	COLUMN	Name of the column of the data object.

Note that we have to define attributes only for the *Vector* class – the *Vector Discrete* class inherits these attributes.

Finally, the ClassMet table stores the definitions of classes, their actions, and the methods for implementing actions:

ClassMet table

CLASS	ACTION	METHOD	ACTDESC
Vector	CREATE	_vcreate()	Creates an object of the Vector class
Vector	PRINT	_vprint()	Prints data of an object of the Vector class
Vector Discrete	CREATE	_dcreate()	Creates an object of the Vector Discrete class
Vector Discrete	PRINT	_dprint()	Prints data of an object of the Vector Discrete class

In this simple example we define only two actions for the *Vector* and *Vector Discrete* classes: Create and Print actions. Implementation of the actions is different for these classes despite the subclass/superclass relationship between the vector and vector discrete classes.

Because the object-oriented programming is implemented with the SAS System, we store the tables that form the data dictionary (for example, the Class, ClassMet, and ClassAtr tables) as SAS data sets, and we implement methods as SAS macro programs.

Let's create a new **myvector** object of the *Vector* class. To do this, the **myvector** object should be associated with the *Vector* class in the tables of the data dictionary. This data dictionary has two tables that define statistical objects and all actions that can be performed on these objects.

The StatObj table stores all the information that is necessary for the definition of a new object. The columns of the StatObj table are defined as follows:

Columns of the StatObj table

Column name	Type	Length	Description
STATOBJ	Character	8	Name of the statistical object
CLASS	Character	8	Name of the class
ATTR_NO	Numeric	8	Order number of the class attribute
ATTR_VAL	Character	20	Value of the class attribute

The STATOBJ, CLASS and ATTR_NO columns form the primary key of the StatObj table.

Each new object should be defined in the StatObj table. The definition of the **myvector** object of the *Vector* class in the StatObj table looks like this:

StatObj table

STATOBJ	CLASS	ATTR_NO	ATTR_VAL
myvector	vector	1	cars
myvector	vector	2	mileage

This table defines a new object of *Vector* class. The name of the object is **myvector**. Recall that, for the purposes of this example, we have mentioned only two parameters: the name of the data object (the first value of the ATTR_VAL column) and the name of the column (the second value of the ATTR_VAL column) that produce the **myvector** object. As you can see for this definition, the new statistical object should be produced from the MILEAGE column of the Cars table. The Cars table can be a SAS data set, or it can be any type of data set that the SAS System can access (for example, a table created by a relational database such as Rdb, SYBASE, ORACLE, a spreadsheet table; or an external file).

The StatAct table contains the definition of actions that should be performed on a statistical object. The columns of the StatAct table are defined as follows:

Columns of the StatAct table

Column name	Type	Length	Description
ANALYSID	Character	8	Identification name of designed statistical analysis
ORDER	Numeric	8	Order number
STATOBJ	Character	8	Name of the statistical object.
ACTION	Character	20	Name of the action to be performed
PARAMS	Character	80	Comma-delimited list of parameters

The ANALYSID and ORDER columns form the primary key of the StatAct table.

In order to define actions for the new **myvector** object, you should fill in the StatAct table as follows:

StatAct table

ANALYSID	ORDER	STATOBJ	ACTION	PARAMS
example1	1	myvector	CREATE	myvector
example1	2	myvector	PRINT	

The definitions stored in the StatAct table mean that Create and Print are the actions that you can perform on the **myvector** object.

Actually, each action is performed by a single macro program %ACTION. You will find a detailed description and the code for this program in Chapter 4. Here we just mention that the function of the %ACTION macro program is to find an appropriate method and to apply it to the object.

The %ACTION macro receives three named parameters: `object`, `action`, and `params`. The `object` parameter gets the name of the statistical object to be processed. The `action` parameter gets the name of the action to be applied to the object. The `params` parameter gets a quoted string containing parameters of the action, if any. For example, the creation of the **myvector** object is performed by submitting the following macro:

```
%action(object=myvector, action="Create",
params="myvector");
```

This macro would automatically submit the _vcreate() method (see the ClassMet table) implementing the Create action specifically for the *Vector* class.

Now we will look in greater detail at two aspects of the Create action:

1. Creation of the object is a generic action that exists for each class.

2. Creation of an object requires additional definitions in the Object and Property tables of the data dictionary.

Each time that you want to create a new object, you have to define, in terms of data objects, where and how the data of this object is to be stored. You make this definition in the Object and Property tables.

The Object table lists data objects and the names of corresponding SAS data sets where their data is stored. The Property table specifies the properties of data objects, listing the columns and characteristics (name, type, length, and so on) of each data object.

In our example, we specified that the **myvector** object of the *Vector* class should be produced from the MILEAGE column of the Cars table (see the StatObj table earlier in this chapter). Thus, the Cars table and at least one of its columns, MILEAGE, should be defined in the Object and Property tables, like this:

Object table

OBJECT	DATASET.	TITLE	LIBRARY
cars	cars	Automobile Data Table	automob

Property table (selected columns)

OBJECT	COLUMN	TITLE	TYPE	LENGTH	ATTRIBUT
…	…	…	…	…	…
cars	MILEAGE	Mileage data	N	8	

This definition describes the physical location of the Cars table, and specifies its column (only one in this example). The _vcreate() method of the *Vector* class will take this information and check whether the CARS SAS data set that corresponds to the Cars table exists. If not, an empty data set that corresponds to the definitions in the Object and Property tables will be created. The %_VCREATE macro is available from SAS Institute, through the SAS Online Samples facility (for detailed information, refer to the inside back cover of the book).

Suppose that you need to create a new object of the *Vector Discrete* class, say **newvector**. Again, assume that the *Vector Discrete* class is already defined.

First, we'll define this new object in the StatObj table (see the highlighted rows):

StatObj table

STATOBJ	CLASS	ATTR_NO	ATTR_VAL
myvector	vector	1	cars
myvector	vector	2	mileage
newvector	vector discrete	1	cars
newvector	vector discrete	2	weight

The highlighted rows define a new object of the *Vector Discrete* class. The name of the object is
newvector. For simplicity, let's consider only two parameters of the *Vector Discrete* class: the name
of the table and the name of the column that produces the **newvector** object. According to this definition,
the new statistical object should be produced from the WEIGHT column of the Cars table.

In order to define actions for the **newvector** object, you should add to the StatAct table the following
definition (highlighted rows):

StatAct table

ANALYSID	ORDER	STATOBJ	ACTION	PARAMS
example	1	myvector	Create	myvector
example	2	myvector	Print	
example	3	newvector	Create	newvector

The definition that is stored in the third row of the StatAct table means that the new object **newvector**
should be created by the Create action.

As it is defined in the StatObj table, the **newvector** statistical object should be produced from the WEIGHT
column of the Cars table. Thus, you should update the Property table like this (highlighted row):

Property table (selected columns)

OBJECT	COLUMN	TITLE	TYPE	LENGTH	ATTRIBUT
...	...	...	...	...	...
cars	MILEAGE	Mileage data	N	8	
cars	WEIGHT	Weight of a car	N	8	

After you have finished all the definitions, you should submit the following macro:

```
%action(object=newvector, action = "Create",
params="newvector");
```

to create the **newvector** object of the *Vector Discrete* class.

As you can see, an object-oriented approach that is implemented through a table-driven environment provides a mechanism that allows one macro program, for example %ACTION, to be re-used to process many different classes of objects. Such a macro is called a *generic* macro, and it calls appropriate methods, in turn, for each object that it processes. For example:

```
%action(object=newvector, action="Create",
params="newvector") ;
```

is a matching method for object **newvector**, class *Vector Discrete,* and macro _dcreate(). The object itself contains information about which class it corresponds to.

Consider another example, a statistical class: *Hypothesis Testing.* This is a class of objects that results from performing a test that relates to statistical inference. An object of the *Hypothesis Testing* class represents a test through the estimation of a test statistic given null and alternative hypotheses and a confidence level. The methods that are used in estimating these test statistics vary from classical to robust and nonparametric approaches. You want to be able to create objects of the *Hypothesis Testing* class. Such an object may be implemented as a list (see Chapter 2) with the following attributes:

Attribute	Description
statistic	the value of the test statistic, with a NAMES attribute indicating its null distribution.
parameters	the parameters of the null distribution of the statistic.
p-value	the p-value for the test under the null hypothesis.
estimate	an estimate of the corresponding population parameters about which you formulated a null hypothesis. The attributes estimate has a names attribute describing its elements.
null-value	the value of the population parameter that is specified by the null hypothesis. The attribute component null-value has a names attribute describing its elements.
alternative	the value of the input argument alternative: "greater", "less", or "two-sided".
method	the name of the test used.
data name	the name of the input data object.

Introduction to Object-Oriented Statistical Analysis

In statistical analysis it's quite natural to operate by classes, because statistical methods are always linked to data. The advantages of object-oriented statistical programming and analysis are not evident when you are doing a very simple statistical analysis. The advantages arise when you are designing a complex statistical analysis that will perform similar, but not identical, operations on a variety of data objects. By specifying classes of data objects for which identical effects will occur, you can define a single generic macro function that embraces the similarities across object classes, but permits individual implementations (methods) for each defined class.

For example, PROC MEANS produces simple univariate descriptive statistics for numeric variables, and if you type the following:

```
proc means data = v_examp mean ;
var var1 ;
run ;
```

you expect SAS to calculate the mean of the var1 variable according to the discrete numeric type of this variable. However, suppose that you also want to calculate the mean of the var1 variable as an integer value. In order to get what you want, you have to write a simple DATA step as follows:

```
data _null_ ;
        retain mean 0 ;
        set v_examp nobs = last;
        mean = mean + var1 ;
        if _n_ = last then do ;
                mean = int(mean/last + 0.5) ;
                put "Mean of Var1 = " mean ;
        end ;
run ;
```

Such a DATA step must be modified every time a new class of objects is created. Using an object-oriented approach, you can use truly generic methods; they do not have to be modified to accommodate new classes of objects. The objects carry their own methods with them. Thus, when you create a class of objects, you can also create a set of methods to specify how these objects will behave with respect to a certain generic statistical operation.

As an example, let's consider the way that SAS will compute means for continuous and discrete numeric variables using the generic %ACTION macro. If you call the following macro:

```
%action(object=newvector, action="mean");
```

then the %ACTION macro computes the mean of the **newvector** object as a discrete value, because the **newvector** object is of the *Vector Discrete* class. By contrast, in this case:

```
%action(object=myvector,  action="mean");
```

the same macro computes the mean as a continuous value, because the **myvector** object belongs to the *Vector* class.

The %ACTION generic macro program evaluates tables of the data dictionary such as ClassMet, ClassAtr, StatObj, StatAct, Object, and Property; identifies the class of the object and its attributes; finds the appropriate method; and invokes the macro program implementing this method that, finally, processes data stored in the SAS data set.

Because data exists in the statistical object as a reference to an application table, it is possible to use the same application table for different objects. Even the same column of an application table can be referred to in different statistical objects.

For example, if you want to consider the WEIGHT column of the Cars table (shown below) once as a discrete vector and once as a continuous numeric vector, you should define two statistical objects referring to the same data object. Look at the definition of the **r_vector** object in the StatObj table (highlighted rows):

StatObj table

STATOBJ	CLASS	ATTR_NO	ATTR_VAL
myvector	vector	1	cars
myvector	vector	2	mileage
newvector	vector discrete	1	cars
newvector	vector discrete	2	weight
r_vector	vector	1	cars
r_vector	vector	2	weight

The **newvector** and **r_vector** objects that are defined in the StatObj table will be processed differently, although they refer to the same data object. Thus, if you define desired actions on **newvector** and **r_vector** objects like this :

StatAct table

ANALYSID	ORDER	STATOBJ	ACTION	PARAMS
example1	3	newvector	Create	newvector
example1	4	newvector	Mean	
example1	5	r_vector	Create	r_vector
example1	6	r_vector	Mean	

the results of the "Mean" action may be different for the **newvector** and **r_vector** objects, although the action was performed on the same column (WEIGHT) of the same table (Cars).

Developing Statistical Models

All statistical analysis models attempt to describe the structure or relationships of some objects from which data is derived. Modern statistical analysis provides an extremely rich choice of modeling techniques. The choice of a modeling technique depends on the type and structure of your data and what you want the model to test or explain. The development of statistical models is data dependent. The process of developing a statistical model also depends on whether you follow a hypothesis-driven approach (confirmatory data analysis) or data-driven approach (exploratory data analysis). Data analysts frequently combine both approaches.

For example, in classical hypothesis-driven regression analysis, you usually examine residuals using exploratory data analysis methods. The goal of each approach is a model that imitates, as closely as possible, the properties of the real objects being modeled. The differences between model and reality, the residuals, are often the key to reaching a deeper understanding and obtaining a better model. Creating a statistical model usually involves the steps shown in Figure 1:

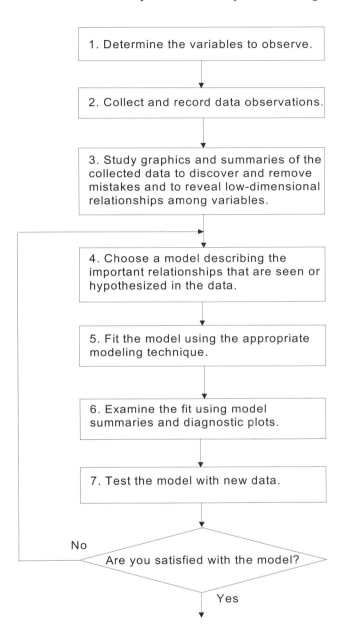

Figure 1.1   Flow chart of the modeling process

At any point in the modeling process described in Figure 1, you may find that your choice of a model does not appropriately fit the data.

In some cases, diagnostic plots (step 6) may give you clues to improve the fit. Sometimes you may need to try transformed variables (step 3) or entirely different variables (step 1). You may need to try different modeling techniques that will allow you to fit in nonlinear relationships or interactions (step 5). At times, all you need is to remove outlying, influential data (step 3), or fit the model robustly (step 5).

Of course, there is no one answer for how to build good statistical models. By iteratively fitting, plotting, testing, changing something, and then refitting, you will arrive at the best fitting model for your data.

When developing a statistical model in the SAS System, there are a wide range of possible modeling techniques to choose from. Among them are generalized linear models, analysis of variance, autoregressive models, and many more. Fortunately, many different classes of statistical models share a substantial common structure. The steps listed in Figure 1.1 apply to many models, and important summaries and diagnostics can be shared directly or adapted straightforwardly from one class of models to another. The object-oriented statistical programming and analyses of the various classes of models take advantage of this common structure.

Data Used for Models

Statistical models allow inferences to be made about objects by modeling associated data, organized by variables. A SAS data set can be considered an object that represents a sequence of observations on some chosen set of variables. SAS data sets allow computations where variables can act as separate objects and can be referenced simply by naming them. This make SAS data sets very useful in modeling.

Variables in SAS data sets are of two types: Numeric and Character. These two types do not cover all data types that you need in statistical modeling. However, by associating a SAS data set variable with some class, you specify how this variable should be considered. For example, associating a numeric variable with the *Vector Discrete* class defines values of this variable as discrete. At the same time, if you associate the same numeric variable with the *Vector* class, the values of this variable will be interpreted as continuous.

When developing a model, the types of data you have are important for deciding which modeling technique best suits your data. Continuous data represents quantitative data having a continuous range of values. Categorical data represents qualitative data (discrete data), meaning that they can assume only certain fixed numeric or character values. In object-oriented statistical analysis you represent categorical data with a factor, which keeps track of the levels or different values that are contained in the data and the level each data point corresponds to. Numeric objects in object-oriented statistical analysis are vectors, or matrices.

A statistical model expresses a response variable as some function of a set of one or more predictor variables. The type of model you select depends on whether the response and predictor variables are continuous or categorical. For example, the classical regression problem has a continuous response and continuous predictors, but the classical analysis-of-variance problem has a continuous response and categorical predictors.

A data property that is very important for statistical modeling and inference is the level of data measurement, or the measurement scale. There are four different scales:

1. Nominal scale: classifies each observation according to specific characteristics. For example, sex (male/female), political party (Democrat/Republican/Independent/Other), binary measures (success/failure).

2. Ordinal scale: classifies each observation according to specific characteristics, but with some ordering. For example, number of cigarettes smoked (0, <1 pack/day, 1–2 packs/day, > 2 packs/day), feelings on an issue (disagree, indifferent, agree), military rank (Captain, Major, Colonel, General).

3. Interval scale: ordering is inherent in the data, and even more importantly, there is a common and constant unit that is used for the measurement. For example, temperature scales such as Celsius or Fahrenheit (but not Kelvin). Zero is not important.

4. Ratio scale: ratios are meaningful, for example 50K is half of 100K. Additional examples include temperature on the Kelvin scale, monetary units, weight, distance, and velocity.

Example of Data Analysis

The example that follows describes only one way of analyzing data through the use of statistical modeling. There is no perfect cookbook approach to building models, as different techniques do different things, and not all of them use the same arguments when doing the actual fitting. The following analysis uses a data set that contains a variety of data for car models. The complete data set is available through the SAS Online Samples facility (for detailed information, refer to the inside back cover of the book).

This is how the data set looks:

Cars table

COUNTRY	TYPE	RELIABIL	MILEAGE	WEIGHT
Japan	Small	5	.	2700
Japan	Medium	5	20	3265
Germany	Medium	.	.	2935
Germany	Compact	.	27	2670
Germany	Compact	4	.	2895
Germany	Medium	.	.	3640
USA	Medium	3	21	2880
USA	Large	3	.	3350
USA	Large	3	23	3325
…	…	…	…	…

Next we show you how to define the statistical analysis of this data using an object-oriented approach. First, let's update information about the **cars** data object in the Property table. The updated table looks like this:

Property table (selected columns)

OBJECT	COLUMN	TITLE	TYPE	LENGTH	ATTRIBUT
…	…	…	…	…	…
cars	COUNTRY	Country	C	20	P
cars	TYPE	Type of a car	C	10	P
cars	RELIABIL	Reliability mark	N	8	
cars	MILEAGE	Mileage data	N	8	
cars	WEIGHT	Weight of a car	N	8	

The value "P" for the ATTRIBUT column of the Property table defines the COUNTRY and TYPE columns as primary key of the Cars table.

Now we can define statistical objects in the StatObj table. Once more, let's assume for simplicity that all statistical classes that we will use in this example are already defined in the tables of the data dictionary, and each of them has only two parameters: data object name and column name. The definitions of the new statistical objects in the StatObj table look like this:

StatObj table

STATOBJ	CLASS	ATTR_NO	ATTR_VAL
mileage	vector	1	cars
mileage	vector	2	mileage
reliabl	vector discrete	1	cars
reliabl	vector discrete	2	mileage
weight	vector	1	cars
weight	vector	2	weight
country	factor	1	cars
country	factor	2	country
type	factor	1	cars
type	factor	2	type

As you see, the definitions of the statistical objects are very obvious and need no additional comments.

Now we are ready to define statistical processing of the new objects. To do it, we just need to define in the StatAct table which actions we want to be done:

StatAct table

ANALYSID	ORDER	STATOBJ	ACTION	PARAMS
example2	1	mileage	Create	mileage
example2	2	reliabl	Create	reliabl
example2	3	weight	Create	weight
example2	4	type	Create	type
example2	5	country	Create	country
example2	6	mileage	Min	
example2	7	mileage	Mean	
example2	8	mileage	Median	
example2	9	mileage	Max	
example2	10	reliable	Mean	
example2	11	reliable	Median	
example2	12	weight	Min	
example2	13	weight	Mean	
example2	14	weight	Median	
example2	15	weight	Max	
example2	16	country	Group	
example2	17	type	Subgroup	

Now the actions will be performed according to the definitions in the StatAct table. You can perform the statistical analysis in the following manner:

1. Create the new statistical objects by using the %ACTION macro as follows:

    ```
    %action(object=mileage, action = "Create",
    params="mileage");

    %action(object=reliabl, action = "Create",
    params="reliabl");

    %action(object=weight, action = "Create",
    params="weight");

    %action(object=type, action = "Create",
    params="type");

    %action(object=country, action = "Create",
    params="country");
    ```

2. Calculate descriptive statistics by using the %ACTION macro as follows:

    ```
    %action(object=reliabl, action = "Median");

    %action(object=weight, action = "Mean");
    ```

The desired descriptive statistics will be calculated – each time by an appropriate method.

However, you should not call the %ACTION macro program for each action. This job will be done for you by the macro program %ANALYZE, which gets the ANALYSID value as its parameter. The %ANALYZE macro is available through the SAS Online Samples facility (for detailed information, refer to the inside back cover of the book).

Summary

In this chapter we recalled the fundamentals of an object-oriented approach and discussed statistical modeling in general terms. The main goal was to demonstrate how to apply this approach to statistical programming and analysis, and how it can be implemented in SAS using a table-driven environment. Briefly, here are the main ideas:

- Specially-structured tables form a data dictionary that enables you to define statistical classes, to define instances of these classes (that is, statistical objects), and to define statistical processing of these instances.

- A mechanism implemented with SAS macro language resolves the definitions stored in the data dictionary.

In the following chapters you will get a detailed explanation of each component in this approach. You will learn how to define statistical classes (Chapter 2) and how to create a set of actions that specify how a statistical object will behave with respect to certain generic operations (Chapter 3). You will learn the structure of the data dictionary and how to define classes and objects in the data dictionary tables (Chapter 4). And finally, you will solve some statistical problems using all you have learned (Chapter 5).

Statistical Objects

Introduction

When using an object-oriented approach in statistical analysis, you think about your data as a statistical object consisting of data along with certain attributes. Your data must be organized into coherent collections having a specific structure. Such a collection is called a data object. In SAS, data objects are just SAS data sets having one or more variables and any number of observations. A statistical object can contain either one data object or several objects and attributes linking (associating) them. For example, if you need to calculate some statistics on an array of values, it's natural to think about the size of the array and the type of its values (continuous or discrete numbers, logical values, and so on.) Why? Because these characteristics influence the kind of calculations. Note that you do not think about data itself – that is, about the specific values of certain variables. You think only about data structure and data type. So, from these characteristics you define a statistical class that your object belongs to.

Statistical classes define the data structure and attributes that are common for the same objects, and they prescribe how these objects should be processed – that is, define class actions. Attributes and actions vary depending on the class. In this chapter we consider some attributes and actions of different classes. All statistical objects (instances of the statistical classes) can be saved, assigned, and edited. Also, each statistical object can be processed by class-specific actions.

Statistical classes form the backbone of object-oriented statistical programming and provide exceptional flexibility in extending the capabilities of SAS.

Statistical classes that we will consider in this and further chapters include vectors, matrices, lists, data tables, factors, and time series. These classes enable us to perform different kinds of statistical analyses. For example:

- Vectors are used for univariate statistical analysis.

- Matrices supply methods for multivariate regression analysis.

- Factors work for analysis of variance.

- Time series support autoregressive, forecasting modeling.

Statistical Classes

Statistical classes can be atomic and complex (non-atomic). An atomic statistical class is based on a single data object and has the attributes of this data object. A complex statistical class unites several statistical classes (both atomic and complex) and has attributes that define relationships among these classes.

Recall that data objects are represented as SAS data sets. A variable of a SAS data set is a specific incidence of a vector, and a set of variables is a specific incidence of a matrix.

This chapter introduces the most basic statistical classes. All are created by generalizing from our simplest statistical class, *Vector*. First we define vectors, then we define matrices, and further we describe data tables. We use vectors to build matrices, and then we generalize matrices to create data tables.

Also, this chapter defines an abstract superclass *Main* that specifies some attributes and actions that are common for all classes derived from it. For example, the *Main* class contains actions that process data dictionary definitions of other classes. The following diagram represents relations among classes:

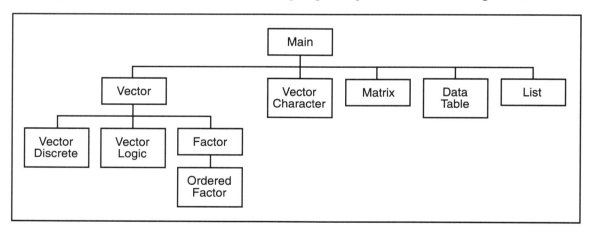

Figure 2.1 Relations among classes

The Vector Class

A vector is simply an array of values. There are several vector classes that differ in data types, and thus differ in their actions of processing and analysis of the vector data. The kinds of values most commonly used in data analysis are: numeric values, logical values, and character strings.

Let's define the following classes: *Vector*, *Vector Discrete*, *Vector Logic*, and *Vector Character*. Because we are operating in the table-driven environment, we will define statistical classes in the Class, ClassAtr, and ClassMet tables of the data dictionary. A detailed explanation of these tables is included in Chapter 4.

Definition of the Vector Class

The *Vector* class operates with an array of continuous numeric values. For example, a **vector** object (the instance of *Vector* class) may consist of numbers:

> 1, 2, -3, 10, 121.2

A special value is used for missing data. It is the convention in SAS to use "." to indicate a missing value in numerical data. The following definition in the Class table describes the *Vector* class:

Class table

CLASS	SPRCLASS	Descript
Vector	Main	Array of continuous numbers

Attributes of the *Vector* class are defined in the ClassAtr table like this:

ClassAtr table

CLASS	ATTR_NO	ATTRNAME	ATTRDESC
Vector	1	OBJECT	Name of the data object producing an object of the Vector class
Vector	2	COLUMN	Name of the column
Vector	3	LENGTH	Number of vector elements
Vector	4	NAMES	Value labels (SAS format name)

The ClassAtr table defines four attributes of the *Vector* class. The OBJECT and COLUMN attributes completely define a data object containing data for an object of the *Vector* class. The LENGTH attribute stores the number of vector elements. Objects of the *Vector* class are identified by referring to the data object and the LENGTH attribute.

The LENGTH attribute can be set in different ways:

- It can be a single number, for example "5", that means that the vector should be created of the first five elements of the data object.

- It can also be a range, for example "12 - 22", meaning that the vector will be composed of the 12th to 22nd elements of the data object.

- It can be set as a list, for example "3 7 23", indicating clearly which elements should compose the vector.

- A mixed form, where range and list are used simultaneously, is also allowed, for example "12 - 22 24 30".

- The LENGTH attribute can be omitted. In this case it will get the value of the real size of the data object specified in the OBJECT and COLUMN attributes.

The NAMES attribute is an optional attribute that is used to associate specific information, such as value labels (SAS formats), with each value of the vector. In the previous chapter you saw several examples of instances of the *Vector* class.

The ClassMet table specifies actions that can be performed on objects of a specific class and implementations (methods) of these actions. This table can be updated each time that a new action is developed for some class, or a better programming implementation for some action is done. In this way you do not have to define and develop all actions for a class at once.

In the previous chapter we looked at definitions of the Create and Print actions for the *Vector* class, which look like this:

ClassMet table

CLASS	ACTION	METHOD	ACTDESC
Vector	CREATE	_vcreate()	Creates an object of the Vector class
Vector	PRINT	_vprint()	Prints data of an object of the Vector class

Let's define two subclasses of the *Vector* class: the *Vector Discrete* and *Vector Logic* classes.

Definition of the Vector Discrete Class

The *Vector Discrete* class operates with an array of discrete numeric values. For example, a **vector** object (an instance of the Vector Discrete class) may consist of numbers:

-10, 2, -3, 10, 12, 102

The *Vector Discrete* class has a lot in common with the *Vector* class, namely:

- the same attributes, although the data differ in type

- the same actions, although the implementation is different.

Thus, we define the *Vector Discrete* class as a subclass of the *Vector* class.

Let's add the definition of the *Vector Discrete* class to the Class table:

Class table

CLASS	SPRCLASS	DESCRIPT
Vector	Main	Array of continuous numbers
Vector Discrete	Vector	Array of discrete numbers

We need not define attributes of the *Vector Discrete* class, as they fully coincide with those of the *Vector* class.

The definition of actions for the *Vector Discrete* class will be defined later in this chapter.

Definition of the *Vector Logic* Class

The *Vector Logic* class operates with an array of logical binary values. For example, a **vector** object (an instance of the *Vector Logic* class) may consist of

TRUE, TRUE, FALSE, TRUE, FALSE, FALSE

or

0, 1,1, 0, 0, 1

or

"Yes", "No", "No", "Yes", "Yes", "No"

Each of these arrays can be considered a set of logical values because their elements can get only one of two values.

The third line in the Class table defines the new *Vector Logic* class:

Class table

CLASS	SPRCLASS	DESCRIPT
Vector	Main	Array of continuous numbers
Vector Discrete	Vector	Array of discrete numbers
Vector Logic	Vector	Array of elements that can get only one of two values

Since the *Vector Logic* class is defined as a subclass of the *Vector* class, the *Vector Logic* class has the OBJECT, COLUMN, LENGTH, and NAMES attributes that you are already familiar with. However, in comparison with the *Vector* and *Vector Discrete* classes, the *Vector Logic* class has some additional attributes. The definition of these attributes in the ClassAtr table looks like this:

ClassAtr table

CLASS	ATTR_NO	ATTRNAME	ATTRDESC
...	...	...	...
Vector Logic	1	TRUEVAL	A value considered TRUE
Vector Logic	2	FALSEVAL	A value considered FALSE

Let's consider two new attributes – TRUEVAL and FALSEVAL. In the two previously defined classes, permitted vector values are implicitly defined by the class name, that is, continuous numeric for the *Vector* class, or discrete numeric for the *Vector Discrete* class. Values of an object of the *Vector Logic* class can be numbers (0,1), or Boolean values (TRUE, FALSE), or character strings ("Yes", "No"), or maybe something else. The TRUEVAL and FALSEVAL attributes enable an object to know its legal values and their logical equivalents, and to be processed by the same methods regardless of values representation.

We will discuss some actions of the *Vector Logic* class later in this chapter.

Definition of the Vector Character Class

The *Vector Character* class operates with character strings. This is an auxiliary class that did not arise from some statistical problem. The **vector** object (an instance of the *Vector Character* class) may consist of several strings:

"Men", "Women", "Boy", "Girl"

We can use this class to store a list of objects. For example, the array

"myvector", "newvector", "r_vector"

contains names of objects that we have defined in Chapter 1.

The last line in the Class table defines this new class.

Class table

CLASS	SPRCLASS	DESCRIPT
Vector	Main	Array of continuous numbers
Vector Discrete	Vector	Array of discrete numbers
Vector Logic	Vector	Array of elements that can get only one of two values
Vector Character	Main	Array of character strings

Attributes of the *Vector Character* class are the same as the attributes of the *Vector* class, and their definitions in the ClassAtr table look like this:

ClassAtr table

CLASS	ATTR_NO	ATTRNAME	ATTRDESC
...	...	...	...
Vector Character	1	object	Name of the data object producing an object of the Vector Character class
Vector Character	2	column	Name of the column
Vector Character	3	LENGTH	Number of vector elements
Vector Character	4	NAMES	Value labels (SAS format name)

Although the *Vector Character* has the same attributes as the *Vector* class, this is not enough to define a relation of superclass/subclass between these classes. In spite of superficial similarities, these classes are entirely different, and there is no place for inheritance between them.

Some actions that we may want to perform on objects of *Vector Character* class might include sorting, extracting values, and replacing values. More detail and discussion about actions on the *Vector Character* class are presented later in this chapter.

The Matrix Class

An important statistical class is the two-way array, or matrix. A matrix object looks like this:

10.1	2.1	3.0
11.0	1.3	3.0
12.1	0.9	4.3
13.2	0.7	0.9
14.6	0.8	9.2

Matrices are used to arrange values of the same type by rows and columns in a rectangular table. For a data analyst, the matrix is a fundamental object, and many statistical procedures analyze data in matrix form. The matrix is also fundamental to mathematical computations such as solving linear equations, computing eigenvalues, and so on.

The matrix object contains values of the same type. This means that you cannot create, for example, a two-column matrix with one column of numeric data and one column of logical data. For statistical analysis, only numeric matrices need to be considered.

Definition of the Matrix Class

The *Matrix* class specifies a two-dimensional table of numeric values and operations. The *Matrix* class is a complex class based on the *Vector* class. Any vector can be turned into a matrix simply by specifying it as an element of the *Matrix* class. We will define the *Matrix* class in the Class table in the following way:

Class table

CLASS	SPRCLASS	DESCRIPT
Vector	Main	Array of continuous numbers
Vector Discrete	Vector	Array of discrete numbers
Vector Logic	Vector	Array of elements that can get only one of two values
Matrix	Main	Array of Vector objects

The attributes of the *Matrix* class are defined in the ClassAtr table like this:

ClassAtr table

CLASS	ATTR_NO	ATTRNAME	ATTRDESC
...	...	...	...
Matrix	1	DIMENSION	List of objects of the Vector class, or name of the Vector Character class that contains list of objects from Vector class producing an objects of the Matrix class
Matrix	2	LENGTH	Number of vector elements

The DIMENSION attribute defines the size of the matrix. This attribute contains one of the following:

- a list of objects of the *Vector* class that compose the matrix

- the name of an object of the *Vector Character* class that in turn contains a list of objects of the *Vector* class. The length of the object of the *Vector Character* class defines the number of matrix columns.

There is no reason to define an object of *Matrix* class that contains a single element. That is why the DIMENSION attribute is interpreted in the following way:

- If there is more than one word in the DIMENSION attribute, this is a list of elements, and each of the elements must be an object of the *Vector* class.

- If there is a single word in the DIMENSION attribute, this must be an object of the *Vector Character* class, that in turn contains names of objects of the *Vector* class only.

Each object of the *Vector* class has its own length. The LENGTH attribute of the *Matrix* class forces the objects of the *Vector* class to have the same length.

As the *Matrix* is the first non-atomic class that we define in the book, let's consider a step-by-step example of how to define an object of this class.

Step 1. Definition of an object of the Matrix class

The definition of new statistical objects is performed in the StatObj table of the data dictionary. Let's define an object that is named **mymatrix** and belongs to the *Matrix* class. Its definition in the StatObj table looks like this:

StatObj table

STATOBJ	CLASS	ATTR_NO	ATTR_VAL
mymatrix	Matrix	1	column1 column2 column3
mymatrix	Matrix	2	20

The first attribute of the *Matrix* class contains a list of objects that produce the **mymatrix** object. The length of such a list is restricted by implementation, that is, by the length of the ATTR_VAL column of the StatObj table (the specific definition and implementation of the data dictionary tables will be considered in Chapter 4).

The value "20" of the second attribute defines the number of rows of the matrix.

Step 2. Definition of objects of the Vector class

Let's define objects of the *Vector* class that compose our mymatrix object:

StatObj table

STATOBJ	CLASS	ATTR_NO	ATTR_VAL
...	...	...	...
column1	Vector	1	data1
column1	Vector	2	age
column2	Vector	1	data2
column2	Vector	2	weight
column3	Vector	1	data2
column3	Vector	2	height

Three objects of the *Vector* class are defined now. The **column1** object is produced from the AGE column of the Data1 data object (SAS data set), while two other objects – **column2** and **column3** – are produced from the WEIGHT and HEIGHT columns of the Data2 data object (SAS data set).

Of course, Data1 and Data2 objects should be defined in the Object table like this:

Object table

OBJECT	DATASET	TITLE	LIBRARY
data1	demogrph	Demographic data about population	populatn
data2	medical	Medical data about population	populatn

Their columns should be defined in the Property table like this:

Property table (selected columns)

OBJECT	COLUMN	TITLE	TYPE	LENGTH	ATTRIBUT
...	...	...	...	....	...
data1	AGE	Age	N	8	
data2	WEIGHT	Weight	N	8	
data2	HEIGHT	Height	N	8	

The **column1**, **column2**, and **column3** objects of the *Vector* class are independent of the **mymatrix** object. They can be processed and analyzed as they are.

Let's consider the advantages of defining the matrix.

- You never need to store your data more than once, because statistical objects do not contain data, but just refer to it. That enables you to create different objects from the same data and analyze them independently.

- Any time you want to change the contents of a *Matrix* class, you only have to update a value of the first attribute of the *Matrix* class. In our example, it is enough to replace the "column1 column2 column3" list with a "myvector r_vector" list, and you will get a new matrix with another dimension and composed of different objects (that were defined in Chapter 1).

Note that SAS does not support storing data in the full matrix form, which includes the names of the columns and of the rows. In the simplest form, a matrix is represented as a SAS data set, where variables represent columns and observations represent rows. The names of the variables can be interpreted as the names of the columns. But we still have no names for the rows.

Factor and Ordered Factor Classes

In data analysis, many kinds of data are qualitative rather than quantitative or numeric. If observations can be assigned only to a category, rather than given a specific numeric value, they are termed qualitative or categorical. The following presents some examples of categorical variables:

gender, where the values are "male" and "female"

status, where the values might be "single", "married", "separated", "divorced"

Categorical data is represented with the statistical class called *Factor*. If an order can be defined on the categorical data, they are represented by the *Ordered Factor* class. The following presents some examples of ordered categorical data:

satisfaction, where the values are "bad", "normal", "good"

knowledge, where the values are "slight", "low", "satisfactory", "excellent"

The Definition of the Factor Class

The *Factor* class in the Class table can be defined as shown here:

Class table

CLASS	SPRCLASS	DESCRIPT
Factor	Vector	Array of categorical values

Since the *Factor* class is a kind of vector, we define it as a subclass of the *Vector* class. Naturally, it has all the attributes of the *Vector* class: OBJECT, COLUMN, LENGTH, and NAMES. But a factor should also keep track of the various levels or categorical values contained in the data, and match an appropriate level for each data point. For this purpose, there must be an attribute that lists valid categorical values (or levels). This additional attribute of the *Factor* class can be defined in the ClassAtr table in the following way:

ClassAtr table

CLASS	ATTR_NO	ATTRNAME	ATTRDESC
...	...	...	...
Factor	1	LEVELS	A list of valid values, or a name of the Vector Characater object containing legal values.

The LEVELS attribute will store different levels of a factor, and it can be set in two ways:

- When the number of different levels is quite small, the LEVELS attribute can be assigned a list of values, for example, "male" and "female". The size of the list is limited by implementation. We include this issue in the discussion about the data dictionary in Chapter 4.

- Another way to assign the LEVELS attribute is to specify the name of an object of the *Vector Character* class that contains all levels of the factor. This object is defined the same way as for an object of the *Matrix* class (see "Definition of the Matrix Class" earlier in this chapter). If you operate with data organized according to relational rules, you will find a data object that contains a list of all valid values (factor levels).

Definition of the Ordered Factor Class

The *Ordered Factor* class in the Class table can be defined as shown here:

Class table

CLASS	SPRCLASS	DESCRIPT
Ordered Factor	Factor	Array of ordered categorical values

The *Ordered Factor* class inherits attributes and actions from the *Factor* class. However, the LEVELS attribute has an additional feature: it defines not only a list of valid values, but also their order. Thus, the list of values for the *Ordered Factor* class will be sorted in ascending order by level. In this way, the LEVELS attribute defines relationships between different levels of a factor.

The *Factor* and *Ordered Factor* classes are a natural form for categorical data in object-oriented statistical programming, and specific actions can be developed for these classes.

The objects from the *Factor* and *Ordered Factor* classes are represented in SAS as variables of a SAS data set.

The Data Table Class

A class that is very similar to *Matrix* is the *Data Table* class. Up to this point, all the described statistical objects contained data of only one type. An object of the *Data Table* class consists of rows and columns of data, just like a matrix, except that the columns can be of different types. This difference is significant − it leads to a difference in interpretation and in analysis of objects. Despite the similarity between the *Matrix* and *Data Table* classes, we cannot define relations of inheritance between them.

The following is an example of an object of the *Data Table* class. The first column consists of character values, the next three columns are numeric, and the last column is logical.

Man	1	20	178	TRUE
Man	1	23	168	FALSE
Woman	1	18	178	TRUE
Man	2	32	1181	TRUE

Data tables are data objects that are designed primarily for data analysis and modeling. The idea of a data table is to group data by variables regardless of their type. You can think of them as generalized matrices.

Data tables generalize the type aspect of a matrix. Matrices can be of only one type, but data tables allow you to change types from column to column. So the main benefit of a data table is that it allows you to mix data of different types into a single object for analysis and modeling.

Definition of the Data Table Class

We will define the Data Table class in the following way:

Class table

CLASS	SPRCLASS	DESCRIPT
...		
Matrix	Main	Array of Vector objects
...		...
Data Table	Main	Array of one-dimensional objects

According to this definition, the *Data Table* class can be composed of different objects that are represented as a one-dimensional array. It means that the objects of the *Vector*, *Vector Character*, and *Ordered Factor* classes, for example, can compose objects of the *Data Table* class.

The definition of attributes of the *Data Table* class looks very similar to that of the *Matrix* class:

ClassAtr table

CLASS	ATTR_NO	ATTRNAME	ATTRDESC
...	...	...	...
Matrix	1	DIMENSION	List of objects of the Vector class, or name of the Vector Character object that contains list of Vector objects producing the Matrix object
Matrix	2	LENGTH	Number of vector elements
...	...	...	...
Data Table	1	DIMENSION	List of one-dimensional objects, or name of the Vector Character object that contains list of one-dimensional objects producing the Data Table object
Data Table	2	LENGTH	Number of object elements

The difference is that the DIMENSION attribute of the *Data Table* class can contain names of different objects, not just objects of the *Vector* class.

The List Class

The objects of the *List* class are the most generic and the most flexible objects for holding data. The *List* class is a non-atomic class and allows you to combine objects of different types into a single object. An object of the *List* class is an ordered collection of components, and each component of a *List* object can be any data object. The components of such an object can be different types and sizes. Thus, from component to component, the type and class of the object can change. For example, an object of the *List* class might have three components consisting of a vector of character strings, a matrix of numbers, and another object of the *List* class. Hence, the *List* class objects are more general than objects of the *Vector* or *Matrix* classes because they can have components of different classes, and they are more general than objects of the *Data Table* class because they are not restricted to having a rectangular structure (rows and columns).

Definition of the List Class

The definition of the *List* class is very general:

Class table

CLASS	SPRCLASS	DESCRIPT
...		
List	Main	Array of objects

The *List* class has a single attribute:

ClassAtr table

CLASS	ATTR_NO	ATTRNAME	ATTRDESC
...	...	...	...
List	1	DIMENSION	List of different objects, or name of the Vector Character object that contains a list of objects producing an object of the List class

The DIMENSION attribute defines a *List* class's components. This is equivalent to specifying a list, where each value is an entire data object.

We assume that an object of the *List* class always contains more than one object. So, if the DIMENSION attribute contains a single word, this is interpreted as a name of an object that must be of the *Vector Character* class. If the DIMENSION attribute contains more than one word, this is interpreted as a list of different objects.

Objects of the *List* class can be represented as several SAS data sets linked together.

Attributes

Attributes specify characteristics of statistical objects. Every statistical object receives a CLASS attribute simply by being defined, that is, the name of the class that the object belongs to. This attribute is shared by all statistical objects, and it is called an *implicit* attribute. This is the most important attribute, because it defines a new statistical object and prescribes how other attributes must be interpreted and evaluated. For example, the LENGTH attribute of the *Vector* class is quite different from that of the *Matrix* class. This attribute is also used to call appropriate actions for a specific statistical object. Because of its special role in the definition of an object, CLASS is called a *defining* attribute. All statistical classes inherit this attribute from the *Main* class.

All atomic classes have OBJECT and COLUMN attributes that refer to data objects. At the same time, non-atomic classes have no OBJECT or COLUMN attributes, because they never refer to any data object, but only to statistical objects. This is one way to distinguish between atomic and non-atomic classes.

There are some attributes that must be assigned a value, but one which may not be set manifestly. We have previously discussed the LENGTH attribute of the *Vector* class. This attribute will get an obligatory value, although it may not be set explicitly.

Some attributes may not require a value. For example, the NAMES attribute of the *Vector* class does not require a value to be assigned. These attributes are optional.

In Chapter 1 we have used the term *generic action* (action that is common for different classes). For all classes we define the action View, which enables us to view attributes. Each class has a specific method for implementing the View action. The View action gets information from the data dictionary table for each class, and then displays it in the format for that specific class.

You are already familiar with the %ACTION macro introduced in Chapter 1 (for a detailed description and code, see Chapter 4). To view attributes of some object, you must submit the %ACTION macro with two parameters: the name of the object and the name of the action. For example, you can view all attributes of the **myvector** object by submitting the following:

```
%action(object=myvector, action="View");
```

As a result the following information will be printed:

```
OBJECT:      MYVECTOR
CLASS:       VECTOR
ATTRIBUTES:
OBJECT = CARS, COLUMN = MILEAGE, LENGTH = 105, NAMES =
```

For some classes, the View action performs some kind of examination. For example, this action enables you to examine factor levels for the *Factor* class. Let's assume that we have defined the **service** object of the *Ordered Factor* class. We can submit the %ACTION macro like this:

```
%action(object=service, action="View");
```

The printed output will look like this:

```
OBJECT:      SERVICE
CLASS:       ORDERED FACTOR
ATTRIBUTES:
OBJECT = SERVICE, COLUMN = ESTIMATN, LENGTH = 325, NAMES = ,
LEVELS = "BAD"(1) "SATISFACTORY"(2) "NORMAL"(3) "GOOD"(4)
"EXCELLENT"(5) -- TOTAL 5 LEVELS
```

As you see, this output provides you with a summarization of the values of the factors, their levels, and total quantity.

The View action is implemented recursively. If we have an object that belongs to a non-atomic class, the View action will give us information about this object and about all objects constructing this one. Let's consider how the View action will work for the **mymatrix** object of the *Matrix* class. You should submit the following macro:

```
%action(object=mymatrix, action="view");
```

You will get this output:

```
OBJECT:      MYMATRIX
CLASS:       MATRIX
ATTRIBUTES:
DIMENSION = COLUMN1 COLUMN2 COLUMN3, LENGTH = 20
```

```
OBJECT:          COLUMN1
CLASS:           VECTOR
ATTRIBUTES:
OBJECT = DATA1, COLUMN = AGE, LENGTH = 53, NAMES =

OBJECT:          COLUMN2
CLASS:           VECTOR
ATTRIBUTES:
OBJECT = DATA2, COLUMN = WEIGHT, LENGTH = 53, NAMES =

OBJECT:          COLUMN3
CLASS:           VECTOR
ATTRIBUTES:
OBJECT = DATA2, COLUMN = HEIGHT, LENGTH = 53, NAMES =
```

The implementation of the View action for different classes is available through the SAS Online Samples facility (for detailed information, refer to the inside back cover of the book).

Processing Data in Statistical Objects

Once a statistical object is defined in the tables of the data dictionary, we can start to use it. The statistical class that the object belongs to defines which actions can be done on this object. Recall that actions of each class are listed in the ClassMet table; this table also specifies which method implements each action. Thus, each object knows which action can be called for that object, and which method implements this action.

We can divide actions in two groups: *preparing* and *analyzing* actions. Actions that do not produce statistical results but do something with an object will be called preparations. Actions that do provide you with some statistical results or inference will be called analyzing actions. This division is not a strong one. We will show you further that there are some actions that simultaneously prepare an object and perform some statistical analysis. In this chapter we will consider actions that are closer to preparations. Chapter 3 contains discussion of analyzing actions.

You already know that in order to perform any action, you just submit the %ACTION macro with name of the object and name of the action. For example, to print the contents of the **myvector** object, just write:

```
%action(object = myvector, action  = "Print");
```

It is common to start from the Create action.

The Create Action

Create is a generic action because it exists for each class. This action does the following:

1. checks correctness of the statistical object definition

2. creates the statistical object.

Note that the Create action does not deal with data but with the definitions in the table of the data dictionary. The implementation of this action differs from class to class. It is important to mention that the Create action is implemented recursively. That is, when you create an object of the *Matrix* class, you recursively create objects of the *Vector* class that comprise the matrix.

Let's consider how the Create action works for an object of the *List* class. Suppose we need to create a **new_list** object of the *List* class and it consists of a **new_matr** object of the *Matrix* class, a **new_char** object of the *Vector Character* class, and a **new_tab** object of the *Data Table* class. The **new_matr** object consists, in turn, of **v1**, **v2**, and **v3** objects of the *Vector* class. The **new_tab** object consists of a **v4** object of the *Factor* class and a **v5** object of the *Vector Character* class. The Create action for the **new_list** object works in the following way:

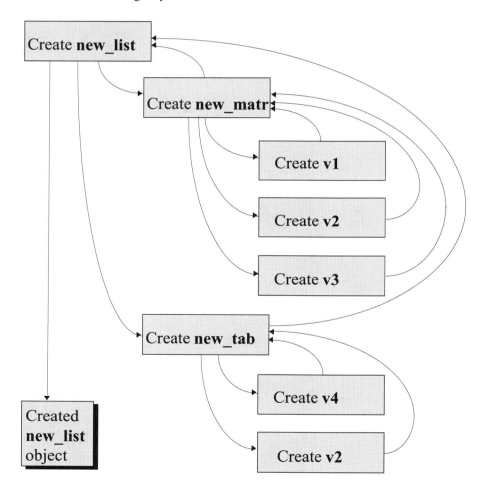

Figure 2.2 The recursive nature of the Create action

Implementation of the Create action is discussed in Chapter 4.

Now let's see how each statistical object is being created.

Creating Vectors

We have six one-dimensional classes: *Vector*, *Vector Discrete*, *Vector Logic*, *Vector Character*, *Factor*, and *Ordered Factor*. The definition of the Create action for these classes appears in the ClassMet table like this:

ClassMet table

CLASS	ACTION	METHOD	ACTDESC
Vector	CREATE	_vcreate()	Creates an object of the Vector class
Vector Discrete	CREATE	_dcreate()	Creates an object of the Vector Discrete class
Vector Logic	CREATE	_bcreate()	Creates an object of the Vector Logic class
Vector Character	CREATE	_ccreate()	Creates an object of the Vector Character class
Factor	CREATE	_fcreate()	Creates an object of the Factor class
Ordered Factor	CREATE	_ocreate()	Creates an object of the Ordered Factor class

The implementations of the Create action for all of these classes have much in common. The code of these macro programs is available through the SAS Online Samples facility (for detailed information, refer to the inside back cover of the book).

Creating Matrices

Matrix is a non-atomic class. An object of the *Matrix* class consists of several objects of the *Vector* class. So, the Create action of the *Matrix* class checks the correctness of the object definition and performs the Create action for all vectors constructing the matrix. The definition of this action for the *Matrix* class looks like this:

ClassMet table

CLASS	ACTION	METHOD	ACTDESC
...	...	...	...
Matrix	CREATE	_mcreate()	Creates an object of the Matrix class

The %_MCREATE macro program implementing this action is discussed in detail in Chapter 4.

Creating Data Tables

Data Table is also a non-atomic class that is produced from several one-dimensional classes. The Create action is recursively performed for all objects combining a data table. The definition of the Create action for the *Data Table* class looks like this:

ClassMet table

CLASS	ACTION	METHOD	ACTDESC
...	...	...	...
Data Table	CREATE	_tcreate()	Creates an object of the Data Table class

The %_TCREATE macro program implementing this action is available through the SAS Online Samples facility (for detailed information, refer to the inside back cover of the book).

Creating Lists

It is now clear that the *List* is a non-atomic class, and thus the Create action is recursively performed for all objects combining the list. The definition of the Create action for the *List* class looks like this:

ClassMet table

CLASS	ACTION	METHOD	ACTDESC
...	...	...	...
List	CREATE	_lcreate()	Creates an object of the Data Table class

The %_LCREATE macro program implementing this action is available through the SAS Online Samples facility (for detailed information, refer to the inside back cover of the book).

The View Action

View is a generic action, because it is defined for all classes. We have already discussed this action in "Attributes" earlier in this chapter. Here we just have to define this action for classes:

ClassMet table

CLASS	ACTION	METHOD	ACTDESC
Main	View	_vview()	Reports attributes of an atomic object
Factor	View	_fview()	Reports attributes of an object of the Factor class
Ordered Factor	View	_oview ()	Reports attributes of an object of the Ordered Factor class
Matrix	View	_mview()	Reports attributes of an object of the Matrix class
Data Table	View	_tview()	Reports attributes of an object of the Data Table class
List	View	_lview()	Creates an object of the Data Table class

Note that because the *Main* class is a superclass for the *Vector*, *Vector Discrete* class, and so on, the View action is inherited by the objects belonging to these classes. The implementation of the View action for *Factor*, *Ordered Factor*, *Matrix*, *Data Table*, and *List* is different for each class.

The source code of these macro programs is available through the SAS Online Samples facility (for detailed information, refer to the inside back cover of the book).

Preparing Data

Statistical analysis is iterative by nature. A statistician or data analyst uses data not only as input to some statistical or calculating procedure, but also as a source for additional information. With each new clue from the data, the analyst can repeat some steps of analysis using the new information.

During data pre-analysis, you can get information about outlying observations (data points) or observations having missing values. Deletion of outlying observations is not always correct because they are not necessarily bad observations. If they are correct, they may be very informative points in the data. For example, they may indicate that the data did not come from a normally distributed population. On the other hand, if there are bad observations, corrective actions may include correction of errors in the data, deletion of outlying observations, redesigning the experiment, or collecting more data.

In preparing data for analysis, we may want to group the data according to some criterion, or we may want to sort the data. Such general preparatory steps can be handled by several actions.

The "Missing" action drops observations having missing values from the object. This action gets one parameter:

```
element     name of the object element that must be processed.
```

The Outlier action detects and processes outliers. For example, outliers can be detected by comparing the studentized residuals to a critical value of a *t*-distribution that is chosen using a Bonferroni-type adjustment. This action gets four parameters:

`element`	name of the object element that must be processed.
`cr_value`	can be a critical p-value or any cut-off value.
`criteria`	studentized residuals or standardized residuals.
`operatn`	operation that must be done on outliers. It can be "drop" for extracting, or "interpol" for linear interpolation.

The Sort action sorts the object. This action gets two parameters:

`by`	name of the object element that is used as sorting key.
`order`	sorting order, which can be "asc" for ascending and "desc" for descending order.

The Extract action performs conditional extraction of data from the object. This action gets four parameters:

`element`	name of the object element that must be processed.
`conditn`	logical expression that must be applied to data of the object element.
`operatn`	operation that should be done on data meeting the condition. It can be "keep" or "drop".
`outobj`	name of the object that contains results of the Extract action – usually of the same class as an element that defined in the element parameter.

We can now define actions for the statistical classes. Our comments are included where the action implementation has some peculiarity. Unless we specify otherwise, the code for all macro programs implementing class actions is available through the SAS Online Samples facility (for detailed information, refer to the inside back cover of the book).

Preparing Data in the Vector Classes

For one-dimensional statistical classes we define the following actions:

ClassMet table

CLASS	ACTION	METHOD	ACTDESC
...	...	...	...
Vector	MISSING	_vmiss()	Extracts missing values from an object of the Vector class
Vector	OUTLIER	_vout()	Processes outliers of an object of the Vector class
Vector	SORT	_vsort()	Sorts an object of the Vector class
Vector	EXTRACT	_vextr()	Conditional extraction of data from an object of the Vector class
Vector Discrete	MISSING	_dmiss()	Extracts missing values from an object of the Vector Discrete class
Vector Discrete	OUTLIER	_dout()	Processes outliers of an object of the Vector Discrete class
Vector Discrete	SORT	_dsort()	Sorts an object of the Vector Discrete class
Vector Discrete	EXTRACT	_dextr()	Conditional extraction of data from an object of the Vector Discrete class
Vector Logic	MISSING	_bmiss()	Extracts missing values from an object of the Vector Logic class
Vector Logic	SORT	_bsort()	Sorts an object of the Vector Logic class
Vector Logic	EXTRACT	_bextr()	Conditional extraction of data from an object of the Vector Logic class
Vector Character	MISSING	_cmiss()	Extracts missing values from an object of the Vector Character class
Vector Character	SORT	_csort()	Sorts an object of the Vector Character class
Vector Character	EXTRACT	_cextr()	Conditional extraction of data from an object of the Vector Character class
Factor	MISSING	_fmiss()	Extracts missing values from an object of the Factor class
Factor	SORT	_fsort()	Sorts an object of the Factor class
Factor	EXTRACT	_fextr()	Conditional extraction of data from an object of the Factor class
Ordered Factor	MISSING	_omiss()	Extracts missing values from an object of the Ordered Factor class
Ordered Factor	SORT	_osort()	Sorts an object of the Ordered Factor class
Ordered Factor	EXTRACT	_oextr()	Conditional extraction of data from an object of the Ordered Factor class

Note that the Outlier action is implemented only for *Vector* and *Vector Discrete* classes.

The Sort action for the *Ordered Factor class*, as opposed to all the other classes, performs sorting according to the levels associated with values, but not according to the values themselves.

The Extract action enables you to apply a condition to each vector value. The condition is written as if it is the right side of the logical expression. For example, if you want to drop all negative values from the **myvector** object, you should define this in the StatAct table like this:

StatAct table

ANALYSID	ORDER	STATOBJ	ACTION	PARAMS
example1	1	myvector	Create	myvector
example1	2	myvector	Print	
example1	3	myvector	Extract	, <0, drop

Or, submit the %ACTION macro like this:

```
%action(object= myvector, action = "Extract", params= ",< 0,
drop");
```

Preparing Data in the Matrix Class

For the *Matrix* class you define only the Extract action:

ClassMet table

CLASS	ACTION	METHOD	ACTDESC
...	...	...	...
Matrix	Extract	_mextr()	Conditional extraction of data from an object of the Matrix class

Execution of the Extract action for the *Matrix* class is quite different from that of one-dimensional classes. This action enables you to define a condition for an entire row or column. The `element` parameter gets the "row" or "column" value. Using the "row" value means that the logical expression is applied to rows. Likewise, the "column" value applies the logical expression to columns. The `conditn` parameter contains the logical expression that is applied to rows or columns. The value of the `operatn` parameter is also applied to the whole row or column that meets the logical condition. For example, earlier in this chapter we defined the **mymatrix** object, which is composed of three vectors (**column1**, **column2**, and **column3**) and has 20 rows. If we want to drop from our matrix all columns containing only 0 values, we would define this in the StatAct table as follows:

StatAct table

ANALYSID	ORDER	STATOBJ	ACTION	PARAMS
...	...	...	...	...
example2	1	mymatrix	CREATE	mymatrix
example2	2	mymatrix	EXTRACT	column1, =0, drop

You obtain the same result by submitting the %ACTION macro like this:

```
%action(object= mymatrix, action = "Extract", params= "column1,= 0,
drop");
```

The ability to perform more comprehensive conditions can be easily achieved with user-written macro functions in the `conditn` parameter.

Preparing Data in Data Table

For the Data Table class you define the following actions:

ClassMet table

CLASS	ACTION	METHOD	ACTDESC
...	...	...	...
Data Table	SORT	_tsort()	Sorts an object of the Data Table class
Data Table	EXTRACT	_textr()	Conditional extraction of data from an object of the Data Table class

The Sort action is implemented in such a way as to preserve the data table's entire relations. The `by` parameter gets the name of an object of one-dimensional class combining the data table. When a value of this object is moved, it is moved together with values from other objects that share the same row. It works just like the SAS sorting procedure, PROC SORT.

The implementation of the Extract action for the *Data Table* class is similar to that of one-dimensional classes. It simply applies the Extract action to one of the objects comprising the data table. The difference is the following: when some value should be dropped, it is dropped together with values from other objects that share the same row. In other words, it is dropped together with the whole row of the data table.

Let's consider an example, where the **my_dt** object of the *Data Table* class contains the **myvector** object of the *Vector* class. Assume that you want to drop all negative values from the **myvector** object. In order to save all of the relations in the data table, you must drop the values from the **myvector** object together with corresponding values of other objects combining the data table. The Extract action will do it for us, if you submit the %ACTION macro like this:

```
%action(object= my_dt, action = "Extract", params= "myvector,< 0,
drop");
```

Summary

In this chapter we defined several statistical classes, their attributes, and some of their actions. In the next chapter we deal with statistical generic actions. We will create a set of actions that specify how different statistical objects behave with respect to a certain generic action. We will then demonstrate reusable SAS macro programs performing generic statistical actions in SAS.

CHAPTER 3
Statistical Programming

Introduction

This chapter is addressed to those who would like to see statistical programming in SAS implemented with classes and actions that form the core of object-oriented technology. The challenge here is to help you create new applications for data analysis while preserving a simple view of the SAS macro language.

Development of Generic Actions

The object-oriented approach provides a mechanism that readily allows one action to be applied to many different classes of objects. If some action is common in its goal for different objects, we call it generic. A generic action takes an object as an argument, and the nature of the object determines how this action is carried out. The actual actions are performed by methods that carry out the specific implementation for a particular class. Thus, applying the generic action to objects of different classes produces the results designed for these classes, automatically.

Implementation of generic actions in SAS as macro functions tends to be very simple, thanks to the table-driven environment.

The table-driven environment consists of a data dictionary and the programs that support it. In Chapter 4 we describe the data dictionary and its structure. The concept and implementation of the table-driven environment is described in *Table-Driven Strategies for Rapid SAS Applications Development*.

Typically, generic actions can be implemented in SAS with a single macro function that evaluates tables of the data dictionary in order to determine the class of the object, finds the appropriate method, and invokes the macro implementing this method. As a SAS user, you should never need to explicitly call a method; generic actions provide the interface you need for most purposes. This interface has the following features:

- Users of generic actions can expect the actions to adapt to new classes of objects without any intervention from the user.

- Designers of new classes of objects can redefine generic actions by writing a method, that is, a new function with the same arguments as defined for the generic action.

In Chapter 2 we defined several statistical classes and considered such generic actions as Create, Print, and Extract. In this chapter we concentrate on statistical instances of these classes, which provide a conceptual basis for more complex statistical classes that are defined later.

The statistical classes defined up to now do not assume knowledge of modeling or sophisticated statistical analysis. But this level of generalization is sufficient to perform preliminary statistical analysis. Each basic statistical object can be analyzed before it is included into the more complex statistical model.

Let's consider the calculation of descriptive statistics for the basic statistical classes that we have defined in Chapter 2. The generic action Descriptive will carry out these calculations.

The Descriptive Action

The Descriptive action is a generic action that calculates descriptive statistics for objects of different classes and creates a new object that contains the results. It also enables you also to calculate statistics by groups. The Descriptive action has three parameters:

element   name of the object element that must be processed.

by   name of the object element that is used as grouping key.

outobj   name of the output object containing results.

The element and by parameters are not used by one-dimensional classes.

The outobj parameter is an optional parameter containing the name of the output object created by the Descriptive action. The class of this object depends on the analyzed object. The outobj parameter can get a name of the object of the appropriate class that is already defined in the StatObj table, and then the permanent output object is created according to this definition. Also, the outobj parameter can be omitted, in which case the results are just printed.

Now let's see how this action is implemented for different classes.

Descriptive Statistics for Vectors

For five one-dimensional classes (*Vector, Vector Discrete, Vector Logic, Factor, Ordered Factor*) we define the Descriptive action in the ClassMet table like this:

ClassMet table

CLASS	ACTION	METHOD	ACTDESC
Vector	DESCRIPTIVE	_vdescr()	Calculates descriptive statistics for the Vector class
Vector Discrete	DESCRIPTIVE	_ddescr()	Calculates descriptive statistics for the Vector Discrete class
Vector Logic	DESCRIPTIVE	_bdescr()	Calculates descriptive statistics for the Vector Logic class
Factor	DESCRIPTIVE	_fdescr()	Calculates descriptive statistics for the Factor class
Ordered Factor	DESCRIPTIVE	_fdescr()	Calculates descriptive statistics for the Ordered Factor class

Implementation of the Descriptive action is quite different for each of the one-dimensional classes. First of all, it depends on the type of data. We have already considered differences in calculating averages for discrete and continuous numerical values. These differences are reflected in the macro programs implementing the Descriptive action. For example, if you want to analyze the **myvector** object, you must submit the following macro:

```
%action(object=myvector, action="Descriptive");
```

In this case, the %ACTION macro program examines the **myvector** object, discovers that it is of the *Vector* class, and submits %_VDESCR macro program as an implementation of the Descriptive action, as it is defined in the ClassMet table above.

Before we describe the methods implementing the Descriptive action for different classes, we should mention that the methods do not use `element` and `by` parameters. These parameters are redundant for one-dimensional objects.

In order to store the results of the Descriptive action, we have to define a class that describes objects that are intended to store the calculated statistics. Let's call this class *Vector Statistics* and define it in the Class table like this:

Class table

CLASS	SPRCLASS	DESCRIPT
Vector Statistics	Main	Descriptive statistics of an object of the one-dimensional class

This class has three attributes that specify the name and columns of the data object where the statistics are stored. These attributes are defined in the ClassAtr table like this:

ClassAtr table

CLASS	ATTR_NO	ATTRNAME	ATTRDESC
Vector Statistics	1	OBJECT	Name of the data object that stores statistics
Vector Statistics	2	STATNAME	Name of the element that contains the name of the statistics
Vector Statistics	3	STATVAL	Name of the element that contains a value of the statistics

The OBJECT attribute must be of the *Data Table* class containing two objects of the *Vector Character* class.

The element that is defined in the STATNAME attribute must be stored as a column of character type and 20 bytes length. The element that is defined in the STATVAL attribute should be stored as a column of character type and 80 bytes in length. Although in most cases statistics are represented by numerical values, we allow for the use of character variables, which are often useful. For example, one of the things that the output object should contain is the name of the processed object. This can be stored as a pseudo-statistic named OBJECT, keeping the name of the processed object. Finally, the results are stored in the SAS data set as shown in the following table:

Newres table

NAME	VALUE
OBJECT	myvector
NOBS	1345
N	1307
NMISS	38
MIN	55.789
MAX	72.564

Of course, the output object will contain statistics appropriate to the processed statistical object.

We can define at least two generic actions for the *Vector Statistics* class, the Create action and the Print action. The methods that implement these actions are defined in the ClassMet table of the data dictionary as follows:

ClassMet table

CLASS	ACTION	METHOD	ACTDESC
Vector Statistics	CREATE	_vscreat()	Creates an object of the Vector Statistics class
Vector Statistics	PRINT	_vsprint()	Prints data of an object of the Vector Statistics class

The %_VSCREAT and %_VSPRINT macro programs are available through the SAS Online Samples facility (for detailed information, refer to the inside back cover of the book).

If you want to store the results of the Descriptive action permanently, you have to define an object of the *Vector Statistics* class in the StatObj table. Let's consider an example of definition of such an output object, named **results**. Its definition in the StatObj table will look like this:

StatOjb table

STATOBJ	CLASS	ATTR_NO	ATTR_VAL
results	Vector Statistics	1	newres
results	Vector Statistics	2	name
results	Vector Statistics	3	value

Of course, the **newres** data object with the appropriate columns NAME and VALUE must be defined in the Object and Property tables of the data dictionary. The NAME should be defined as a column of character type and 20 bytes length, and the VALUE should be defined as a column of character type and 80 bytes length.

Now, if you submit the following macro program:

```
%action(object=myvector, action="Descriptive",
params=" , , results");
```

the descriptive statistics calculated for the **myvector** object are stored in the SAS data set corresponding to the **newres** data object.

%_VDESCR macro program

The %_VDESCR macro program calculates descriptive statistics for continuous numerical values. This macro is straightforward and can use SAS procedures, such as PROC UNIVARIATE, for example. The following statistics are calculated for objects of the *Vector* class:

NOBS	the number of observations
N	the number of observations on which the calculations are based
NMISS	the number of missing values
MIN	the smallest value
MAX	the largest value
RANGE	the difference between the largest and the smallest value, that is, MAX - MIN
MEAN	average of N observations
VAR	the variance
STD	standard deviation
MODE	the most frequent value (If there is more than one mode, the smallest mode is used.)
SUM	the sum of the N observations
KURTOSIS	the kurtosis statistic
SKEWNESS	the skewness of the data
P1	the first percentile
P5	the fifth percentile
P10	the tenth percentile
Q1	the lower quartile, or twenty-fifth percentile
MEDIAN	the median, or fiftieth percentile
Q3	the upper quartile, or seventy-fifth percentile
QRANGE	the difference between the upper and lower quartiles, that is, Q3 - Q1
P90	the ninetieth percentile
P95	the ninety-fifth percentile
P99	the ninety-ninth percentile

The %_VDESCR macro program does the following:

1. From the StatObj table of the data dictionary, it gets information about the data object producing the object of the *Vector* class.

2. From the Object and Property tables of the data dictionary, it gets information about the name of the SAS data set and its location.

3. It generates an appropriate call to PROC UNIVARIATE, and executes it.

4. It creates an output object of the *Vector Statistics* class, or prints the results.

The code for this macro program is shown below.

```
/*
PROGRAM          _VDESCR
DESCRIPTION      Calculation of descriptive statistics for an
                 object of the Vector class
USAGE            %_vdescr (object, outobj) ;
PARAMETERS       object — the name of the statistical object of
                 the Vector class

                 outobj — the name of the statistical object of
                 the Vector Statistics class containing
                 calculated descriptive statistics
REQUIRES         The &libwork is a global macro variable
                 defining the _SA_WORK library that contains
                 statistical objects
AUTHORS          T.Kolosova and S.Berestizhevsky.

*/
%macro _vdescr (object, outobj) ;
%if %upcase(&object) = NULL %then
%do ;
    %if &outobj ^= %then
    %do ;
/*
Creates an output object of the Vector Statistics class
*/
%action(object= &outobj, action = "Create", params
 = "&outobj") ;
/*
Calculates descriptive statistics
/*
    proc univariate data = &libwork..&object noprint ;
    var &object ;
    output out = _out_
    n = n
    nobs = nobs
    nmiss = nmiss
    min = min
    max = max
    range = range
    mean = mean
    var = var
    std = std
    mode = mode
    sum = sum
    kurtosis = kurtosis
    skewness = skewness
    p1 = p1
    p5 = p5
    p10 = p10
    q1 = q1
    q3 = q3
    median = median
    qrange = qrange
    p90 = p90
    p95 = p95
```

```
        p99 = p99 ;
        run ;

        proc transpose data = _out_  out = _out1_ ;
        run ;

        data _out_ (keep = name value) ;
            length name $20 value $80 ;
            set _out1_ ;
            if _n_ = 1 then do ;
                name = "object" ;
                value = "&object" ;
                output ;
            end ;
            name = _label_ ;
            value = col1 ;
            output ;
        run ;
/*
Writes descriptive statistics into the output object of the
Vector Statistics class
*/
        %action(object= &outobj, action = "Put Elements",
                params = "_out_,  name, value") ;

    %end ;
    %else
    %do ;
        proc univariate data = &libwork..&object ;
        var &object ;
        run ;
    %end ;
%end ;
%mend ;
```

%_DDESCR macro program

The %_DDESCR macro program calculates descriptive statistics for discrete numeric values. In this case, the calculations must distinguish between discrete and continuous types of data. The %_DDESCR macro program calculates the same statistics for objects of the *Vector Discrete* class as the %_VDESCR macro program calculates for objects of the *Vector* class. In order to calculate these statistics, we can adapt and use SAS facilities. The output of this macro program is either produced as an object of the *Vector Statistics* class, or it is printed.

The %_DDESCR macro program does the following:

1. obtains information about the data object producing the object of *Vector Discrete* class from the StatObj table of the data dictionary

2. obtains information about the name of the SAS data set and its location from the Object and Property tables of the data dictionary

3. generates an appropriate call to PROC UNIVARIATE, and executes it

4. corrects the results of PROC UNIVARIATE so that they reflect the discrete nature of the data (for example, mean)

5. creates the output object of the *Vector Statistics* class, or prints the results.

The following is the code for this macro program:

```
/*
   PROGRAM         _DDESCR
   DESCRIPTION     Calculation of descriptive statistics for an
                   object of the Vector Discrete class
   USAGE           %_ddescr (object, outobj) ;
   PARAMETERS      object - the name of the statistical object
                   of the Vector Discrete class

                   outobj - the name of the statistical object
                   of the Vector Statistics class containing
                   calculated descriptive statistics
   REQUIRES        The &libwork is a global macro variable
                   defining the _SA_WORK library that contains
                   statistical objects
   AUTHORS         T.Kolosova and S.Berestizhevsky.
*/
%macro _ddescr (object, outobj) ;
%if %upcase(&object) = NULL %then
%do ;
*/
  Creates an output object of the Vector Statistics class
/*
%action(object= &outobj, action = "Create", params
  = "&outobj") ;
/*
  Calculates descriptive statistics
*/
        proc univariate data = &libwork..&object noprint ;
        var &object ;
        output out = _out_
        n = n
        nobs = nobs
        nmiss = nmiss
        min = min
        max = max
        range = range
        mean = mean
        var = var
        std = std
        mode = mode
        sum = sum
        kurtosis = kurtosis
        skewness = skewness
        p1 = p1
        p5 = p5
        p10 = p10
        q1 = q1
        q3 = q3
        median = median
        qrange = qrange
        p90 = p90
        p95 = p95
        p99 = p99 ;
        run ;

        proc transpose data = _out_  out = _out1_ ;
        run ;

        data _out_ (keep = name value) ;
           length name $20 value $80 ;
           set _out1_ ;
           if _n_ = 1 then do ;
              name = "object" ;
              value = "&object" ;
              output ;
           end ;
           name = _label_ ;
```

```
/*
   Corrects the results of PROC UNIVARIATE so that they reflect
   the discrete nature of the data
*/
        if upcase(_name_) = "MEAN" then
           col1 = int(col1) ;
        value = col1 ;
        output ;
     run ;
/*
   Writes descriptive statistics into the output object of the
   Vector Statistics class
*/
     %action(object= &outobj, action = "Put Elements",
             params = "_out_, name, value") ;

%end ;
%mend ;
```

%_BDESCR macro program

The %_BDESCR macro program is created for the *Vector Logic* class to calculate TRUE and FALSE values. The output of this macro program is produced either as an object of the *Vector Statistics* class, or it is printed.

The %_BDESCR macro program:

1. obtains information about the data object producing the object of the *Vector Logic* class from the StatObj table of the data dictionary

2. obtains information about the name of the SAS data set and its location from the Object and Property tables of the data dictionary

3. calculates TRUE and FALSE values

4. creates the output object of the *Vector Statistics* class, or prints the results.

The implementation of this program is very simple, and you can write it yourself. Our version of this program is available through the SAS Online Samples facility (for detailed information, refer to the inside back cover of the book).

%_FDESCR macro program

The %_FDESCR macro program implements the Descriptive action for both the *Factor* and *Ordered Factor* classes. This macro program calculates the number of cases for each level. This program is quite similar to %_BDESCR macro program. The difference is that there can be more than two levels of a factor. The code for this program is available through the SAS Online Samples facility (for detailed information, refer to the inside back cover of the book).

Descriptive Statistics for Data Tables

For the *Data Table* class we define the Descriptive action as follows:

ClassMet table

CLASS	ACTION	METHOD	ACTDESC
...	...	...	...
Data Table	DESCRIPTIVE	_tdescr()	Calculates descriptive statistics for the Data Table class

The implementation of the Descriptive action for the *Data Table* class is based on the fact that objects of the *Data Table* class are composed of objects of one-dimensional classes. In simple cases, the %_TDESCR macro program decides which method should be called for an object combining the data table and executes it. In addition, the *Data Table* class enables you to calculate descriptive statistics for grouped data.

The %_TDESCR macro program requires the `element` parameter in order to know the column on which to operate. The `element` parameter gets the name of the one-dimensional object that represents a column of the data table. This object cannot be an object of the *Vector Character* class, because there is no Descriptive action for this class.

The `by` parameter is optional. It may get the name of the one-dimensional object that represents one of the data table's columns. This object can be of the *Vector Discrete*, *Vector Logic*, *Factor,* or *Ordered Factor* classes only.

Suppose you have defined the **my_dt** object of the *Data Table* class, which includes, among others, the **myvector**, **newvector**, and **r_vector** objects. These three objects were defined in Chapter 1. Recall that the **myvector** and **r_vector** objects belong to the *Vector* class, and the **newvector** object belongs to the *Vector Discrete* class. If you want to group all rows of the **my_dt** object by values of the **newvector** object, and then calculate descriptive statistics for the **myvector** object inside these groups, you should submit the following macro:

```
%action(object=my_dt, action="Descriptive",
params="myvector, newvector");
```

The `params` parameter of the %ACTION macro contains a quoted string with `element` and `by` parameters for the Descriptive action. In this example, the `outobj` parameter is not assigned a value, and so the results are simply printed.

The `outobj` parameter can get a name of the object that belongs to the *Table Statistics* class.

Definition of the Table Statistics Class

The *Table Statistics* class describes objects that will store results of the Descriptive action performed on the object of the *Data Table* class. Its definition in the Class table looks like this:

Class table

CLASS	SPRCLASS	DESCRIPT
Table Statistics	Main	Descriptive statistics of an object of the Data Table class

The *Table Statistics* class has four attributes that are defined in the ClassAtr table like this:

ClassAtr table

CLASS	ATTR_NO	ATTRNAME	ATTRDESC
Table Statistics	1	OBJECT	Name of the data object that stores statistics
Table Statistics	2	BYGROUP	Name of the element that contains values of the grouping key
Table Statistics	3	STATNAME	Name of the element that contains a name of the statistics
Table Statistics	4	STATVAL	Name of the element that contains a value of the statistics

The element that is defined in the `bygroup` attribute must be stored as a column of character type and 40 bytes in length. This should be enough to store any grouping value. The element that is defined in the STATNAME attribute must be presented as a column of character type and 20 bytes in length. The element that is defined in the STATVAL attribute should be stored as a column of character type and 80 bytes in length. Finally, the results are stored in the SAS data set similar to the following table:

Results table

BYGROUP	STATNAME	STATVAL
.	OBJECT	my_dt
.	ELEMENT	myvector
male	NOBS	658
male	N	640
male	NMISS	18
male	MIN	55.789
male	MAX	68.356
female	NOBS	687
female	N	667
female	NMISS	20
female	MIN	57. 896
female	MAX	72.564

We now define the Create and Print generic actions for the *Table Statistics* class. The methods that implement these actions are defined in the ClassMet table of the data dictionary like this:

ClassMet table

CLASS	ACTION	METHOD	ACTDESC
Table Statistics	CREATE	_tscreat()	Creates an object of the Table Statistics class
Table Statistics	PRINT	_tsprint()	Prints data of an object of the Table Statistics class

The code for %_TSCREAT and %_TSPRINT macro programs are available through the SAS Online Samples facility (for detailed information, refer to the inside back cover of the book).

The use of the output object is the same as for the one-dimensional classes. If the `outobj` parameter gets the name of the object, which is defined in the StatObj table, the results of the Descriptive action are stored permanently. If the `outobj` parameter gets no value, the results are printed.

%_TDESCR macro program

The %_TDESCR macro program implements the Descriptive action for the *Data Table* class. It does the following:

1. from the StatObj table of the data dictionary, obtains information about the objects producing the data table

2. from the same StatObj table, obtains information about the data objects producing the objects defined in the `element` and `by` parameters

3. obtains information about the names and locations of the relevant SAS data sets from the Object and Property tables

4. creates a temporary SAS data set that contains two objects defined in the `element` and `by` parameters and sorted according to the object of the by parameter

5. generates a call to an appropriate method for calculating descriptive statistics, and executes it

6. creates an output object of the *Table Statistics* class, or prints the results.

The following is the code for this macro program:

```
/*
PROGRAM          _TDESCR
DESCRIPTION      Calculation of descriptive statistics for an
                 object of the Data Table class
USAGE            %_tdescr (object, element, by, outobj) ;
PARAMETERS       object - the name of the statistical object of
                 the Data Table class
                 element - the name of the object element that
                 must be processed
                 by - the name of the object element that is
                 used as grouping key
                 outobj - the name of the statistical object of
                 the Table Statistics class containing
                 calculated descriptive statistics
REQUIRES         The &libwork is a global macro variable
                 defining the _SA_WORK library that contains
                 statistical objects
AUTHORS          T.Kolosova and S.Berestizhevsky.
*/
%macro _tdescr(object, element, by, outobj) ;

%if %upcase(&object) ^= NULL %then
%do ;
    %if &outobj ^= %then
    %do ;
        %action(object= &outobj, action = "create",
                params = "&outobj") ;
        proc sort data = &libwork..&object out = &object;
        by &by;
        run;

        proc univariate data = &object noprint ;
        var &element ;
        by &by;
        output out = _out_
            n = n
            nobs = nobs
            nmiss = nmiss
            min = min
            max = max
            range = range
            mean = mean
            var = var
            std = std
            mode = mode
            sum = sum
            kurtosis = kurtosis
            skewness = skewness
            p1 = p1
            p5 = p5
            p10 = p10
            q1 = q1
            q3 = q3
            median = median
            qrange = qrange
            p90 = p90
            p95 = p95
            p99 = p99 ;
        run ;
```

```
        proc transpose data = _out_  out = _out1_ ;
        var &element ;
        by &by;
        run ;

        data _out_ (keep = &by name value) ;
           length name $20 value $80 ;
          set _out1_ ;
          if _n_ = 1 then do ;
             name = "object" ;
             value = "&object" ;
             output ;
             name = "element" ;
             value = "&object" ;
             output ;
          end ;
          name = _label_ ;
          value = col1 ;
          output ;
        run ;

        %action(object= &outobj, action = "Put Elements",
                params = "_out_, &by, name, value") ;

      %end ;
      %else
      %do ;
        proc univariate data = &libwork..&object ;
        var &element ;
        by &by;
        run ;
      %end ;
    %end ;
  %mend ;
```

The SAS macro programs that we have demonstrated for you up to now are fairly simple and straightforward. And so it should be, since the object-oriented approach should help simplify programming and analysis. The roots of this simplicity and logic lie in the concise and well-thought-out design of statistical classes.

Example Of Designing A New Class And Its Actions

The class/action mechanism allows a consistent implementation of statistical analysis. The statistician who designs a statistical class needs to consider the internal structure for the data. The data analyst should see only the conceptual structure of data. Actions for the class must be written with a clear understanding of which structure is being used.

The ANOVA Class

The new statistical class that we are going to design is the *ANOVA* class, defined as shown below:

Class table

CLASS	SPRCLASS	DESCRIPT
ANOVA	Main	Analysis of variance

This class is based on the *Data Table* class. In order to accent the statistical meaning of the *Data Table* class in this usage, we use the term *observation* to refer to the rows of a data table.

The attributes of this class are defined like this:

ClassAtr table

CLASS	ATTR_NO	ATTRNAME	ATTRDESC
ANOVA	1	DATATAB	Name of the object of the Data Table class.
ANOVA	2	CLASSIF	Names of the classification elements
ANOVA	3	FREQ	Name of the frequency element
ANOVA	4	WEIGHT	Name of the weights element

This table defines four attributes of the *ANOVA* class.

The DATATAB attribute contains the name of the object belonging to the *Data Table* class. All further attributes are based on this object, which should therefore contain all the data that are needed to perform analysis of variances.

The CLASSIF attribute contains names of the elements of the object (defined in the DATATAB attribute) that can serve as classifiers. Recall that the elements of the *Data Table* class are defined as one-dimensional classes. A classification element can be an object that belongs to either the *Vector Discrete*, *Vector Logic*, *Factor,* or *Ordered Factor* class.

The FREQ attribute defines an element that contains frequencies for each observation. It means that each observation of the data table represents several observations in the experiment. An element that is defined in the freq attribute contains a value for each observation that prescribes how many times this observation must be repeated. If this value is missing, the observation is not used in the analysis. The FREQ attribute can get the name of an object of *Vector Discrete* class only.

The WEIGHT attribute defines an element that contains a weight for each observation. If this value is zero, the observation is not used in the analysis. The WEIGHT attribute can get the name of an object of the *Vector* class only.

The ANOVA Action

Now let's define the ANOVA action, which performs an analysis of variance on experimental data. This action analyzes the variance in the values of a continuous response variable as measured for several levels of classification variables. The ANOVA is an example of a non-generic action because it is possible only for a specific class.

The ANOVA action is designed to work on both balanced and unbalanced data. Just remember that "balanced data" means that there are the same number of response observations for each combination of levels of classification variables. The methods that process balanced and unbalanced data are different. The ANOVA action will distinguish which type of data has an object of the *ANOVA* class, and it will use the appropriate statistical method.

The ANOVA action has the following parameters:

`model`	names the dependent variables and independent effects
`class`	gets "yes" or "no" value that tells whether to use classification variables in the analysis
`by`	name of the object element that is used as grouping key
`weight`	gets "yes" or "no" value that tells whether to use weighting or not
`outobj`	name of the object that contains results of the ANOVA action

The `model` parameter of the ANOVA action enables you to specify main effects, crossed effects and nested effects. We have developed the ANOVA action so that it conforms to the SAS convention of model definition.

Main effects are represented by the independent variables themselves, such as **a b c**.

Crossed effects are represented by two variables joined by an asterisk, such as **a*c b*d**.

Nested effects are represented by listing class variables in parentheses after a main or crossed effect, such as **a(b d) c*f(d)**.

Of course, **a**, **b**, **c**, and so on are only the objects from those defined in the CLASSIF attribute during the definition of the object of the *ANOVA* class.

These main, crossed, and nested effects are used in the definition of the model. The model is defined according to the following rule:

<independent variable> = <effects>

for example:

y = a*c b*d

Here, **y** is the object of the *Vector* class that is contained by the object of the *ANOVA* class.

The `by` parameter enables you to obtain separate analysis in groups. This parameter can get the name of the one-dimensional object of the *Vector Discrete*, *Vector Logic*, *Factor*, or *Ordered Factor* class only. Of course, this one-dimensional object must be contained by the object of the *ANOVA* class.

The ANOVA action produces the following results:

PREDICTED	predicted values
RESIDUAL	residuals, calculated as ACTUAL minus PREDICTED
L95M	the lower bound of a 95% confidence interval for the expected value (mean) of the dependent variable
U95M	the upper bound of a 95% confidence interval for the expected value (mean) of the dependent variable
L95	the lower bound of a 95% confidence interval for an individual prediction (this includes the variance of the error, as well as the variance of the parameter estimates)
U95	the upper bound of a 95% confidence interval for an individual prediction
PRESS	the residual for the nth observation that results from dropping the nth observation from the parameter estimates
RSTUDENT	a studentized residual with the current observation deleted
DFFITS	the standard influence of observation on predicted value
COVRATIO	the standard influence of observation on covariance of betas
STDP	the standard error of the mean predicted value
STDR	the standard error of the residual
STDI	the standard error of the individual predicted value
STUDENT	the studentized residuals, the residual divided by its standard error
COOKD	Cook's D influence statistic
H	the leverage
F	F values
SS	sums of squares
DF	degree of freedom
PROB	probabilities for each model

To store the results of the ANOVA action, we have to define a class that is intended to store the calculated statistics. There are two kinds of results produced by the ANOVA action. Some of the statistics are represented as a single value, for example F, SS, DF, and PROB. Other results are calculated for each observation, for example PREDICTED, RESIDUAL, DFFITS, and so on. The first kind of statistics should be stored in an object of the *Table Statistics* class that we have already defined. The second kind of statistics should be stored in an object of a new class.

Let's call this class *Model Statistics* and define it in the Class table like this:

Class table

CLASS	SPRCLASS	DESCRIPT
Model Statistics	Main	Statistics of an object of the ANOVA class

This class has the following attributes defined in the ClassAtr table:

ClassAtr table

CLASS	ATTR_NO	ATTRNAME	ATTRDESC
Model Statistics	1	OBJECT	Name of the data object that stores statistics
Model Statistics	2	BYGROUP	Name of the element that contains values of the grouping key
Model Statistics	3	ACTUAL	Name of the element that contains actual response value
Model Statistics	4	PREDICTED	Name of the element that contains PREDICTED statistics
Model Statistics	5	RESIDUAL	Name of the element that contains RESIDUAL statistics
Model Statistics	6	L95M	Name of the element that contains L95M statistics
Model Statistics	7	U95M	Name of the element that contains U95M statistics
Model Statistics	8	L95	Name of the element that contains L95 statistics
Model Statistics	9	U95	Name of the element that contains U95 statistics
Model Statistics	10	PRESS	Name of the element that contains PRESS statistics
Model Statistics	11	RSTUDENT	Name of the element that contains RSTUDENT statistics
Model Statistics	12	DFFITS	Name of the element that contains DFFITS statistics
Model Statistics	13	COVRATIO	Name of the element that contains COVRATIO statistics

The element that is defined in the BYGROUP attribute must be represented by a column of character type and 40 bytes in length. The elements that are defined in attributes 3 to 13 must be stored as columns of numeric type.

We want to create an object of the *Model Statistics* class, and then we want to print its data. The methods that implement the Create and Print generic actions for the *Model Statistics* class are defined in the ClassMet table like this:

ClassMet table

CLASS	ACTION	METHOD	ACTDESC
Model Statistics	CREATE	_mscreat()	Creates an object of the Model Statistics class
Model Statistics	PRINT	_msprint()	Prints data of an object of the Model Statistics class

The %_MSCREAT and %_MSPRINT macro programs are available through the SAS Online Samples facility (for detailed information, refer to the inside back cover of the book).

Since the results of the ANOVA action should be stored in two different objects linked together, we need to define the output object belonging to the *List* class and containing both of the following:

- an object of the *Table Statistics* class

- an object of the *Model Statistics* class.

Let's define an **anovares** object to store the results of the ANOVA action. Recall that the *List* class has a single attribute dimension that contains a list of the objects. This sequence of objects can be defined like this:

StatObj table

STATOBJ	CLASS	ATTR_NO	ATTR_VAL
anovares	List	1	tabstat anovstat
tabstat	Table Statistics	1	tabstat
tabstat	Table Statistics	2	group
tabstat	Table Statistics	3	name
tabstat	Table Statistics	4	value
anovstat	Model Statistics	1	anovstat
anovstat	Model Statistics	2	group
anovstat	Model Statistics	3	actual
anovstat	Model Statistics	4	predict
anovstat	Model Statistics	5	residual
anovstat	Model Statistics	6	l95m
anovstat	Model Statistics	7	u95m
anovstat	Model Statistics	8	l95
anovstat	Model Statistics	9	u95
anovstat	Model Statistics	10	press
anovstat	Model Statistics	11	rstud
anovstat	Model Statistics	12	dffits
anovstat	Model Statistics	13	covratio

This table defines the **anovares** object of the *List* class. Let's consider this definition in detail.

- The first attribute of the **anovares** object gets the following list: **tabstat anovstat**, which means that there are two objects – **tabstat** and **anovstat** – combining the **anovares** object.

- The **tabstat** object belongs to the *Table Statistics* class, and it is stored in the data object with the same name. Of course, the **tabstat** data object must be defined in the Object and Property tables of the data dictionary.

- The **anovstat** object belongs to the *Model Statistics* class, and it is stored in the data object with the same name. The **anovstat** data objects must be defined in the Object and Property tables.

If we want to store the results of the ANOVA action permanently, we have to define an output object as shown earlier for the Descriptive action.

The following example demonstrates using of the *ANOVA* class. Let's define the **reliabil** object of the *ANOVA* class. This object is based on the Cars data object that we defined in Chapter 1. The definition of the **reliabil** object in the StatObj table looks like this:

StatOjb table

STATOBJ	CLASS	ATTR_NO	ATTR_VAL
reliabil	ANOVA	1	carstab
reliabil	ANOVA	2	type
reliabil	ANOVA	4	weight
carstab	Data Table	1	reliabil type weight
reliabil	Vector Discrete	1	cars
reliabil	Vector Discrete	2	reliabil
type	Factor	1	cars
type	Factor	2	type
weight	Vector	1	cars
weight	Vector	2	weight

Let's consider this definition more closely:

- The **reliabil** object of the *ANOVA* class consists of the **carstab** object of the *Data Table* class.

- The **carstab** object in turn contains **reliabil**, **type**, and **weight** objects.

- The **reliabil** object is of the *Vector Discrete* class, and it is based on the RELIABIL column of the Cars data object.

- The **type** object is of the *Factor* class, and is it based on the TYPE column of the Cars data object.

- Finally, the **weight** object is of the *Vector* class and is based on the WEIGHT column of the Cars data object.

Now, suppose that we want to estimate the effect that the **type**, weighted by **weight**, has on the **reliabil.**

To perform analysis of variance for **reliabil** object of the *ANOVA* class, you have to perform the ANOVA action with the following parameters:

- The `model` parameter gets the following value: 'reliabil = type'.

- The `by` parameter is omitted.

- The `class` parameter gets a "yes" value, so the ANOVA action uses classification with the **type** object as it is defined in the StatObj table (see the first highlighted row in the StatObj table).

- The `weight` parameter gets a "yes" value, so the ANOVA action uses weighting with the **weight** object as it is defined in the StatObj table (see the second highlighted row in the StatObj table).

- The `outobj` parameter gets the name of the recently defined **anovares** object of the *List* class.

Let's submit the %ACTION macro, which performs the ANOVA action for the desired object:

```
%action(object=reliabil, action="ANOVA",
params="'reliabil=type', yes, ,yes,anovares") ;
```

Another way to perform the same action is to define it in the StatAct table, and then submit the %ANALYZE macro program, which gets the appropriate ANALYSID value as its parameter. The %ANALYZE macro program is available through the SAS Online Samples facility (for detailed information, refer to the inside back cover of the book).

The definition of the described action in the StatAct table looks like this:

StatAct table

ANALYSID	ORDER	STATOBJ	ACTION	PARAMS
...	...	...	...	...
anova_ex	1	reliabl	ANOVA	'reliabil=type',yes, ,yes,anovares
...	...	...	...	...

The %ANALYZE macro program should be submitted like this:

```
%analyze(anova_ex);
```

The method that implements the ANOVA action is defined in the ClassMet table:

ClassMet table

CLASS	ACTION	METHOD	ACTDESC
...	...	...	...
ANOVA	ANOVA	_anova()	Performs analysis of variance for the ANOVA class

The %_ANOVA macro program

The %_ANOVA macro program implements the ANOVA action for the *ANOVA* class and does the following:

1. obtains information about the object of the *ANOVA* class from the StatObj table of the data dictionary
2. selects the method of analysis of variance, suitable for data stored in the object of the *ANOVA* class
3. creates a temporary SAS data set that contains data necessary for the analysis of variance
4. invokes the PROC GLM procedure, and executes it
5. creates an output object of the *List* class containing an object of the *Table Statistics* class and an object of the *Model Statistics* class, or prints the results.

The following is the code for this macro program:

```
/*
  PROGRAM           _ANOVA
  DESCRIPTION       Analysis of variance for the specified model
  USAGE             %_anova (object, model, class, by, weight,
                    outobj) ;
  PARAMETERS        object - the name of the statistical object
                    of the Data Table
                    class model - names the dependent variables
                    and independent effects

                    class - "yes" or "no" value that tells
                    whether to use classification variables in
                    the analysis

                    by - the name of the object element that is
                    used as grouping key

                    weight - "yes" or "no" value that tells
                    whether to use weighting or not

                    outobj - the name of the statistical object
                    of the List class containing results of ANOVA
  REQUIRES          The &libwork is a global macro variable
                    defining the _SA_WORK library that contains
                    statistical objects
  AUTHORS           T.Kolosova and S.Berestizhevsky.
*/
  %macro _anova(object, model, class, by, weight, outobj);

     %if %upcase(&object) = NULL %then
        %goto err_exit ;

     %let model =
     %substr(%bquote(&model),2,%eval(%length(&model)-2)) ;
     %let classif = ;
     %let freq = ;
     %let weight = :

     data _null_ ;
        set &libref..statobj (where=(left(upcase(statobj))
           = upcase(left("&object"))
           and left(upcase(class)) = "ANOVA"));
        if attr_no = 2 then call symput("classif",
     classif);
        if attr_no = 3 then call symput("freq", freq);
        if attr_no = 4 then call symput("weight", weight);
     run;

     proc glm data = &libwork..&object
        %if &outobj ^= %then %do;
           outstat = _stat_ noprint
        %end;
        ;
        %if %upcase(&class) = YES and &classif ^= %then
        %do ;
           class &classif ;
        %end ;

        %if &freq ^= %then %do ;
           freq &freq  ;
        %end ;
        %if %upcase(&weight) = YES and
                    &weight ^= %then %do ;
           weight &weight  ;
        %end ;
```

```
      %if &by ^= %then
      %do ;
         by &by ;
      %end ;
      model &model ;
      %if &outobj ^= %then %do;
         output out = _out_
            P=P
            R=R
            L95M=L95M
            U95M=U95M
            L95=L95
            U95=U95
            STDP=STDP
            STDR=STDR
            STDI=STDI
            STUDENT=STUDENT
            COOKD=COOKD
            H=H
            PRESS=PRESS
            RSTUDENT=RSTUDENT
            DFFITS=DFFITS
            COVRATIO=COVRATIO  ;
      %end;
   run;
   quit;

   %if &outobj ^= %then %do;
      %let actual = %scan(&model,1,=);

      data _out_;
         set _out_ (keep = &actual
            %if &by ^= %then %do;
               &by
            %end ;
            P R L95M U95M L95 U95 STDP STDR STDI STUDENT
            COOKD H PRESS RSTUDENT DFFITS COVRATIO,
            rename = (&actual = actual
            %if &by ^= %then %do;
               &by = bygroup
            %end;
            ));
            if actual ^= . ;
      run;

      data _stat_ (drop = _name_ _source_ _type_);
         set _stat_ (where = (_type_ = "SS1")
            %if &by ^= %then %do;
               rename = (&by = bygroup)
            %end;
            );
      run;
      proc transpose data = _stat_ (drop = _name_
      _source_ _type_)
      out = _stat1_ (rename = (col1 = statval _name_ =
      statname)
         drop = _label_);
         %if &by ^= %then %do;
            by bygroup;
         %end ;
      run;

      %action(object = &outobj,action="Put Elements",
         params="_stat1_,_out_") ;
   %end;
%err_exit :
%mend ;
```

Summary

The main goals of this chapter were to:

- demonstrate how to define generic actions for statistical objects

- demonstrate how to write reusable SAS macro programs for implementing statistical actions.

In the next chapter we show you how to design the table-driven environment (data dictionary and programs supporting it) to store and manage the class definitions.

CHAPTER 4

Data Dictionary for Classes and Actions Definitions

Introduction

Object-oriented statistical programming and analysis is a technique for writing statistical applications. In this technique, application design consists of the definition of data objects, statistical classes, and actions in the tables of a data dictionary.

A data dictionary is a tool that organizes and represents data and its relationships. This tool works like a central card catalog in a library. The thousands of books that a library houses would be difficult to locate and retrieve without first referring to the card catalog. Each card in the centralized catalog contains information about a book, such as author, date of publication, location, and a short summary. In some instances, simply referring to the catalog provides enough information to satisfy a wide variety of inquiries.

In the same way, a data dictionary, provides a centralized facility to control the information resource. Everything about data objects, statistical classes and actions is defined in specially structured tables. Special programs transform data from these tables (metadata) into an appropriate statistical application. Such tables and programs form the table-driven environment.

This chapter explains data dictionary concepts that enable the statistician to make generalizations about statistical objects, classes, and actions. There are many interesting and useful SAS macro programs in this chapter.

The proposed data dictionary is built according to a relational data model. For more information on issues of relational technology, see *Table-Driven Strategies for Rapid SAS Applications Development*, Chapter 2, "The Data Dictionary."

Data Dictionary for Data Objects Definitions

The data dictionary for data objects is the repository of control information such as tables and their columns, column domains, column attributes, formats, and so on. In order to define data objects, we need to build a set of data dictionary tables to contain data about these objects.

Recall that a data object is implemented as a SAS data set, and thus it is characterized by such data set properties as name and location, data set variables, and their characteristics.

We propose a possible set of data dictionary tables that includes five tables: Library, Object, Location, Property, and Link. This set is called the Kernel set, and may be extended by additional tables at any time.

Below we describe the tables of the Kernel set in terms of the relational data model. Data dictionary tables will be referred to as "tables," and application tables will be called "data objects."

The Library Table

The Library table lists SAS library specifications. The columns of the Library table are defined as follows:

Columns of the Library table

Column name	Type	Length	Description
LIBRARY	Character	8	SAS library name
LOCATION	Character	80	Operating-system-specific file name for SAS library

The LIBRARY column is the primary key of the Library table.

The Object Table

The next table is the Object table, which lists data objects and the names of corresponding SAS data sets where their data is stored. The Object table also defines data object titles. The columns of the Object table are defined as follows:

Columns of the Object table

Column name	Type	Length	Description
TABLE	Character	8	Data object name
TITLE	Character	80	Data object title
DATASET	Character	8	SAS data set name where data of the data object is stored

The TABLE column is the primary key of the Object table.

The Location Table

The Location table lists data objects and the SAS libraries where the SAS data sets corresponding to the data objects are kept. The columns of the Location table are defined as follows:

Columns of the Location table

Column name	Type	Length	Description
TABLE	Character	8	Data object name
LIBRARY	Character	8	SAS library name

The TABLE and LIBRARY columns together form the primary key of the Location table.

The Location and Object tables together define physical patterns (SAS data sets) for each data object in several SAS libraries.

The Property Table

The Property table specifies the properties of data objects. The Property table lists the columns and their characteristics. The columns of the Property table are defined as follows:

Columns of the Property table

Column name	Type	Length	Description
TABLE	Character	8	Data object name
COLUMN	Character	8	Column name
TITLE	Character	80	Column title
TYPE	Character	1	Column data type: C - Character or N - Numeric
LENGTH	Numeric	8	Column length
FORMAT	Character	20	SAS format, or user-defined format
ATTRIBUT	Character	2	Column property: P - Primary key and/or I - Index
DOMTAB	Character	8	Domain data object name
DOMCOL	Character	8	Domain column name
MEANTAB	Character	8	Meaning data object name
MEANCOL	Character	8	Meaning column name
PLACE	Numeric	8	Place in the data set
INITVAL	Character	80	Initial column's value
FORMULA	Character	80	Formula for computed column
MISSING	Character	1	Code for a missing value

The TABLE and COLUMN columns together form the primary key of the Property table.

For example, the properties of the Property data object look like this (this example also shows how data dictionary tables store their own definitions):

Property table (selected columns)

TABLE	COLUMN	TYPE	LENGTH	ATTRIBUT	INITVAL
..	...	...	...	...	...
Property	TABLE	C	8	P	
Property	COLUMN	C	8	P	
Property	TITLE	C	80		
Property	TYPE	C	1		
Property	LENGTH	N	8		
Property	FORMAT	C	20		
Property	ATTRIBUT	C	2		
Property	DOMTAB	C	8		
Property	DOMCOL	C	8		
Property	MEANTAB	C	8		
Property	MEANCOL	C	8		
Property	PLACE	N	8		
Property	INITVAL	C	80		
Property	FORMULA	C	80		
Property	MISSING	C	1		
...	...	...	...	...	...

The structure of the Property table supports SAS formats, "meanings," and user-defined dynamic formats (like the values defined through PROC FORMAT).

Meaning

A "meaning" is a simple way to replace an uninformative value with meaningful text. The definition of the meaning for a column is merely a reference to the data object and its column that contains meaningful text. The correct definition of the meaning is based on the relationships between data objects. The column for which we define meaning has to be the foreign key of the data object that contains meaningful text.

Let's consider an example that will show when a meaning is useful.

In Chapter 1 we demonstrated an example of the Cars data object that was defined in the Property table like this:

Property table (selected columns)

OBJECT	COLUMN	TITLE	TYPE	LENGTH	ATTRIBUT
...	...	...	...	....	...
cars	COUNTRY	Country	C	20	P
cars	TYPE	Type of a car	C	10	P
cars	RELIABIL	Reliability mark	N	8	
cars	MILEAGE	Mileage data	N	8	
cars	WEIGHT	Weight of a car	N	8	

You can also see the data of this data object in the "Example of Data Analysis" section in Chapter 1.

The RELIABIL column contains reliability scores. Let's introduce an additional data object that explains the values of reliability scores. This data object, stored in the Category table, may look like this:

Category table

RELIABIL	CATEGORY
.	not estimated
2	not reliable
3	reliable on speed under 65 ml/h
4	reliable on speed under 80 ml/h
5	reliable on curves on speed under 80 ml/h
6	high reliability standard

The following steps show you how to present the values of the Cars data object, where a reliability score is replaced by its meaningful category.

1. Add a definition of the Category data object to the Property table like this:

Property table (selected columns)

OBJECT	COLUMN	TITLE	TYPE	LENGTH	ATTRIBUT
...	...	...	...	....	...
category	RELIABIL	Reliability mark	N	8	P
category	CATEGORY	Reliability category description	C	40	
...	...	...	...	...	...

2. Update the definition of the RELIABIL column of the Cars data object in the Property table like this:

Property table (selected columns)

OBJECT	COLUMN	TITLE	TYPE	LENGTH	MEANTAB	MEANCOL
...	...	...	...	....	...	...
cars	RELIABIL	Reliability mark	N	8	category	CATEGORY

Here we have finished defining the meanings for the RELIABIL column of the Cars data object. From this point, the data dictionary and its programs know how to represent the values of the RELIABIL column. Note that you can easily update the contents of the Category data object, and this change is instantly used to represent values of the RELIABIL column.

User-defined dynamic format

The definition of a user-defined dynamic format is simply the definition of the column domain (a value in terms of PROC FORMAT) and its corresponding meaning (a label in terms of PROC FORMAT).

For instance, in the previous example, the RELIABIL column of the Category data object can serve as domain for the RELIABIL column of the Cars data object. We can define the user-defined dynamic format named CATEGORY. for the RELIABIL column of the Cars data object. During data entry, such a format replaces the reliability scores in the Cars data object with a meaningful category and provides error-free domain data. The definition of this format in the Property table looks like this:

Property table (selected columns)

OBJECT	COLUMN	FORMAT	DOMTAB	DOMCOL	MEANTAB	MEANCOL
...	...	...	...	....	...	...
cars	RELIABIL	CATEGORY.	category	RELIABIL	category	CATEGORY

Indexes

Primary keys and indexes are also defined in the Property table. An index is a column that allows direct access to the rows in a data object (table). Indexes are stored in a separate location from the data in a table. They influence data object update times, because an application updates both data objects and indexes.

The Link table

The Link table specifies pairs of data objects that are linked by foreign keys. The columns of the Link table are defined as follows:

Columns of the Link table

Column name	Type	Length	Description
TABLE	Character	8	Table name
RELTABLE	Character	8	Name of the related table
COLUMN	Character	8	Column name
RELCOL	Character	8	Name of the column from the related table

The TABLE, COLUMN, RELTABLE, and RELCOL columns together form the primary key of the Link table.

Previously we defined the Category data object, which is linked with the Cars data object. Let's see how this link can be defined in the Link table:

Link table

TABLE	RELTABLE	COLUMN	RELCOL
...	...	...	...
cars	category	RELIABIL	RELIABIL
...	...	...	...

In "Example for the Data Analyst" later in this section, there is an example of the definition of a data object in the tables of the Kernel set.

Data Dictionary for Classes and Actions Definitions

The data dictionary for classes and actions is intended to store information about statistical classes, their attributes and actions, and relations between them. In Chapters 2 and 3 we already used the data dictionary tables, prior to their definition. In this section, we will build a set of data dictionary tables that will contain data about statistical classes.

We propose a set of five data dictionary tables: Class, ClassAtr, ClassMet, StatObj, and StatAct. This set is called the Classes set, and its tables should be defined in the Kernel set and handled by the data dictionary.

The Class table

The Class table lists the specifications for the statistical classes. The columns of the Class table are defined as follows:

Columns of the Class table

Column name	Type	Length	Description
CLASS	Character	20	Statistical class name
SPRCLASS	Character	20	Superclass name
DESCRIPT	Character	80	Description of the class

The CLASS column is the primary key of the Class table.

The ClassAtr table

The ClassAtr table specifies attributes of statistical classes. The columns of the ClassAtr table are defined as follows:

Columns of the ClassAtr table

Column name	Type	Length	Description
CLASS	Character	20	Statistical class name
ATTR_NO	Number	8	Attribute order number
ATTRNAME	Character	20	Attribute name
ATTRDESC	Character	80	Description of the attribute

The CLASS and ATTR_NO columns form the primary key of the ClassAtr table.

The ClassMet table

The ClassMet table specifies the actions and methods of statistical classes. The columns of the ClassMet table are defined like this:

Columns of the ClassMet table

Column name	Type	Length	Description
CLASS	Character	20	Statistical class name
ACTION	Character	20	Action name
METHOD	Character	10	Name of the SAS macro program implementing the action
ACTDESC	Character	80	Description of the action

The CLASS and ACTION columns form the primary key of the ClassMet table.

The StatObj table

The StatObj table defines statistical objects – specific instances of statistical classes. The StatObj table contains the following columns:

Columns of the StatObj table

Column name	Type	Length	Description
STATOBJ	Character	8	Name of the statistical object
CLASS	Character	20	Name of the statistical class to which the object belongs
ATTR_NO	Number	8	Order number of the class attribute
ATTR_VAL	Character	80	Value of the class attribute

The STATOBJ, CLASS and ATTR_NO columns form the primary key of the StatObj table.

The StatAct table

The StatAct table is intended to specify action of statistical analysis that should be performed on the statistical object. The columns of the StatAct table are defined as follows:

Columns of the StatAct table

Column name	Type	Length	Description
ANALYSID	Character	8	Identification name of designed statistical analysis
ORDER	Numeric	8	Order number
STATOBJ	Character	8	Name of the statistical object
ACTION	Character	20	Name of the action to be performed
PARAMS	Character	80	Comma-delimited list of parameters

The ANALYSID and ORDER columns form the primary key of the StatAct table.

In the "Example for the Statistician" section there is an example of the definition of statistical classes in the tables of the Classes set.

Examples

By designing statistical classes and actions, the statistician generalizes some specific problem that the data analyst has to solve. The programmer implements actions and their methods for the recently designed statistical classes. At this point the data analyst can use the created statistical classes to solve the specific problem – and other similar problems.

This section shows you how to solve a specific statistical problem by using an object-oriented approach to statistical programming and analysis.

The Cars data object, which was introduced in Chapter 1, contains a variety of data for car models, including type of car, mileage, weight, and so on. Suppose you want to model the effect that weight has on the gas mileage of a car.

We propose the following steps to solve this problem:

1. Study graphics and summaries of the collected data to correct mistakes and to reveal low-dimensional relationships among variables.

2. Fit the model describing the important relationships hypothesized in the data using the appropriate modeling technique.

3. Examine the fit using model summaries and diagnostic plots.

Let's design the statistical classes that enable us to execute these steps.

Example for the Statistician

The new statistical class to be designed is the *Model* class. We'll define this new class in the Class table:

Class table

CLASS	SPRCLASS	DESCRIPT
Model	Main	General linear model

This class has only one attribute, which is defined in the ClassAtr table:

ClassAtr table

CLASS	ATTR_NO	ATTRNAME	ATTRDESC
Model	1	DATATAB	Name of the object of the Matrix class.

The DATATAB attribute contains the name of the object that belongs to the *Matrix* class and that contains data for analysis. Recall that an object of the *Matrix* class is defined as a set of objects of the *Vector* class, and we use it to define new actions.

Let's start by defining the actions. It is easy to do by following the steps defined earlier:

Step 1: Study graphics, correct mistakes and reveal low-dimensional relationships among variables.

There are many graphical techniques that enable visual analysis of variables. We confine ourselves to only a few of them, but you can add as many graphical techniques as you need.

The Histogram Action

Recall that the *Vector* class already has a Descriptive action to calculate univariate statistics and produce an object of the *Vector Statistics* class that contains results of the calculations (see "Development of Generic Actions" in Chapter 3).

Now let's define the Histogram action for the *Vector* class. The Histogram action calculates empirical distribution for objects of the *Vector* class, and it produces results in either graphic or tabular form. This action gets two parameters, which define type of output that is produced:

`outobj`   name of the output object containing results.

`outdev`   name of the output device for the graphical presentation.

The `outobj` parameter contains the name of the output object created by the Histogram action. The class of this object will be discussed further. The `outobj` parameter is optional. It obtains the name of the object of the appropriate class that is already defined in the StatObj table, and then the permanent output object is created according to this definition. If the `outobj` parameter is omitted, the results are just printed in tabular form.

The `outdev` parameter specifies a device for graphical presentation of results, and it is also optional. If the `outdev` parameter is omitted, the results are not presented graphically.

Now let's define the Histogram action in the ClassMet table:

ClassMet table

CLASS	ACTION	METHOD	ACTDESC
Vector	HISTOGRAM	_vhist()	Calculates empirical distribution for the Vector class

In order to store the results of the Histogram action, we define a class that describes objects intended to store the calculated empirical distribution. Let's call this class *Vector Distribution* and define it in the Class table like this:

Class table

CLASS	SPRCLASS	DESCRIPT
Vector Distribution	Main	Empirical distribution of an object of the Vector class

This class has seven attributes that specify the name and columns of the data object where the empirical distribution is stored. These attributes are defined in the ClassAtr table like this:

ClassAtr table

CLASS	ATTR_NO	ATTRNAME	ATTRDESC
Vector Distribution	1	OBJECT	Name of the data object that stores statistics
Vector Distribution	2	LEFTVAL	Name of the column that contains the value of the left limit of an interval
Vector Distribution	3	RIGHTVAL	Name of the column that contains the value of the right limit of an interval
Vector Distribution	4	VALUE	Name of the column that contains the number of observations in the interval
Vector Distribution	5	CUMVALUE	Name of the column that contains the cumulative number of observations in the interval
Vector Distribution	6	FREQ	Name of the column that contains the frequency of observations in the interval
Vector Distribution	7	CUMFREQ	Name of the column that contains the cumulative frequency of observations in the interval

The OBJECT attribute must be of the *Data Table* class containing at least six objects of the *Vector* class.

Finally, the results of the execution of the Histogram action are stored in the data object as illustrated in the following SAS data set:

LEFTVAL	RIGHTVAL	VALUE	CUMVALUE	FREQ	CUMFREQ
...	...	...		...	
-0.367	-0.267	13	22	0.13	0.22
-0.267	-0.167	18	40	0.18	0.40
-0.067	0.033	24	64	0.24	0.64
0.033	0.133	20	84	0.20	0.84
...	...	...		...	

We will consider the implementation of this action in "Example for the Programmer" section.

The Transform Action

Another action that it is useful to add to the *Vector* class is Transform. This action performs different transformations of data to find low-dimensional relationships. There are many possible transformations, and we will consider only a few here. However, from this example, you can extend a list of transformations as needed.

The Transform action applies a specific calculation to an object of the *Vector* class. This action gets two parameters that are defined like this:

```
transform    transformation formula

outobj       name of the output object
```

The `transform` parameter can obtain the following values:

- one of the keywords that are defined for the Transform action and mean specific transformations, for example: LOG for logarithmic transformation, LOGN for log-normal transformation, INV for inverse, and so on

- a formula in SAS syntax, with or without macro functions, where a value of a variable is replaced with #, for example: 1/cos(#).

The optional `outobj` parameter specifies an output object that contains the results of a transformation. This object is also of the *Vector* class. If you define an object of the Vector class in the tables of data dictionary, and specify its name in the `outobj` parameter, the Transform action creates this object and stores the results permanently. If you omit the `outobj` parameter, the Transform action puts the result back to the input object, thus overriding the initial values.

The definition of the Transform action in the ClassMet table looks like this:

ClassMet table

CLASS	ACTION	METHOD	ACTDESC
Vector	TRANSFORM	_vtrans()	Transforms values of an object of the Vector class

The implementation of the Transform action is discussed in detail in "Example for the Programmer" later in this chapter.

The Scatter Plot Action

Consider a two-dimensional scatter plot as a technique for visualizing low-dimensional relationships between variables. This action is defined only for a matrix because scatter plots use variables that have twin correspondence (for example, X, Y coordinates).

The Scatter Plot action produces a two-dimensional graphical representation between two elements of an object of the *Matrix* class. This action requires three parameters, which are defined like this:

axisx   name of the object element that is used for X axis

axisy   name of the object element that is used for Y axis

outdev   name of the output device

The `axisx` parameter names the element of the matrix that will be used as axis X variable.

The `axisy` parameter names the element of the matrix that will be used as axis Y variable.

Together, `axisx` and `axisy` parameters define a pair of the matrix components that have relationships you wish to reveal.

The `outdev` parameter defines an output device, either file or screen.

The definition of the Scatter Plot action of the *Matrix* class looks like this in the ClassMet table:

ClassMet table

CLASS	ACTION	METHOD	ACTDESC
Matrix	SCATTER PLOT	_mplot()	Produces two-dimensional scatter plot

In "Example for the Programmer" later in this chapter we discuss the implementation of this action.

Step 2: Fit the model

The Model Action

Now let's define the Model action that performs the fitting of a model to experimental data. Model is an example of a non-generic action, because it is possible only for a specific class.

The Model action has the following parameters:

model   names the dependent and independent variables

outobj   name of the object that contains results of the Model action

The `model` parameter of the Model action allows you to specify a model that you want to fit. We have developed the Model action so that it conforms to the SAS convention of model definition. You can define a model by naming the dependent variables and independent effects. Some examples of model definitions are shown below.

Specification	Kind of Model
y = x1	simple regression
y = x1 x2	multiple regression
y = x1 x1*x1	polynomial regression
y = a	one-way ANOVA
y = a b c	main effects model
y = a b a*b	main effects with interaction model
y = a b(a) c(b a)	nested model
y = a x1	analysis-of-covariance model
y = a x1(a)	separate-slopes model
y = a x1 x1*a	homogeneity-of-slopes model

The `outobj` parameter defines a name of the object containing the results of the fitting, and it determines which kind of object it must be. This object is optional. If you define this object in the StatObj table of the Classes set of the data dictionary, the results of the Model action are stored permanently. If you omit this parameter, the output results are just printed in the SAS OUTPUT window.

The Model action is defined in the ClassMet table like this:

ClassMet table

CLASS	ACTION	METHOD	ACTDESC
Model	MODEL	_model()	Fits a model

In Chapter 3 we defined the *Table Statistics* and *Model Statistics* classes that are used to store results of the ANOVA action. These classes are also suitable to store results of the Model action. Like the ANOVA action, the Model action produces an object of the *List* class that contains the following two elements:

- an object of the *Table Statistics* class

- an object of the *Model Statistics* class

The object of the *Table Statistics* class contains estimates produced by the Model action:

ESTIMATE   estimated regression coeficients for the model

RMSE   the root mean square error

The following results, produced by the Model action, are stored in the object of the *Model Statistics* class:

PREDICTED	predicted values
RESIDUAL	residuals, calculated as ACTUAL minus PREDICTED
L95M	the lower bound of a 95% confidence interval for the expected value (mean) of the dependent variable
U95M	the upper bound of a 95% confidence interval for the expected value (mean) of the dependent variable
L95	the lower bound of a 95% confidence interval for an individual prediction (this includes the variance of the error, as well as the variance of the parameter estimates)
U95	the upper bound of a 95% confidence interval for an individual prediction
PRESS	the residual for the nth observation that results from dropping the nth observation from the parameter estimates
RSTUDENT	a studentized residual with the current observation deleted
DFFITS	the standard influence of observation on predicted value
COVRATIO	the standard influence of observation on covariance of betas
STDP	the standard error of the mean predicted value
STDR	the standard error of the residual
STDI	the standard error of the individual predicted value
STUDENT	the studentized residuals, the residual divided by its standard error
COOKD	Cook's D influence statistic
H	the leverage

The Model action is more complex than the previously described Histogram and Scatter Plot actions because knowledge of SAS procedures is required to build regression models. The statistician should define at least the main steps of the action and the SAS software procedures that should be used, so that the programmer can write a statistically correct application.

The Model action is implemented with the REG procedure and does the following:

1. It fits linear regression models by least-squares.

2. It creates an output object that contains parameter estimates, optional statistics, and diagnostic measures calculated after fitting the model.

We will discuss the detailed implementation of this action in "Example for the Programmer".

Step 3: Examine the fit

The Model action puts its results into an object of the *List* class. This object, in turn, contains an object of the *Table Statistics* class and an object of the *Model Statistics* class.

The Fit Plot Action

One commonly used graphical approach for assessing the fit of a model is to plot actual data and the predicted values of the model on the same graph. Let's define this action for the *Model Statistics* class:

ClassMet table

CLASS	ACTION	METHOD	ACTDESC
Model Statistics	FIT PLOT	_fitplot()	Examines the fit

Recall that an object of the *Model Statistics* class contains the following information, which can be used to analyze the fit:

ACTUAL	actual response value
PREDICTED	predicted values
RESIDUAL	residuals, calculated as ACTUAL minus PREDICTED
L95M	the lower bound of a 95% confidence interval for the expected value (mean) of the dependent variable
U95M	the upper bound of a 95% confidence interval for the expected value (mean) of the dependent variable
L95	the lower bound of a 95% confidence interval for an individual prediction (including the variance of the error, as well as the variance of the parameter estimates)
U95	the upper bound of a 95% confidence interval for an individual prediction
PRESS	the residual for the nth observation that results from dropping the nth observation from the parameter estimates
RSTUDENT	a studentized residual with the current observation deleted
DFFITS	the standard influence of observation on predicted value
COVRATIO	the standard influence of observation on covariance of betas

This information enables us to produce different types of plots showing, for example

- actual and predicted values with the upper and lower 95% confidence interval for the expected value of the dependent value

- actual and predicted values with the upper and lower 95% confidence interval for an individual prediction

- residuals vs. actual values

- residuals vs. observation number.

The Fit Plot action can build all of these plots. The parameters of this action are:

`axisx` names the object element that is used for the X axis

`axisy` names the object elements that are used for the Y axis

`outdev` name of the output device

The `axisx` parameter is optional. If it is omitted, the number of observations is used for X axis.

The `axisy` parameter can contain a list of elements for Y axis. Since the object of the *Model Statistics* class knows exactly what each column stores, we can use pre-defined rules for plot presentation. For example, actual and predicted values are displayed as dots, while boundaries are presented as thin lines. Actually, all these details can be defined as additional parameters for the Fit Plot action.

Example for the Programmer

The programmer has a special role in the object-oriented approach to statistical programming and analysis. Of course, the programmer is usually involved in writing methods that implement the actions of statistical classes. But the programmer's main role is in the development of the mechanism that takes information from the tables of the data dictionary and supports the execution of actions corresponding to specific statistical objects. This mechanism is implemented by the %ACTION macro program.

%ACTION macro program

The %ACTION macro program works with the contents of the data dictionary tables, but not with the contents of data objects. While the contents of the data dictionary tables can be changed at any time, the structure remains unchanged.

Let's define the parameters of the %ACTION macro program. There are three named parameters:

`object` names the object

`action` names the action

`params` comma-separated list of parameters

The `object` parameter is given the name of the statistical object to be processed. Names of statistical objects must be unique.

The `action` parameter is given the name of the action to be applied to the object.

The `params` parameter is given a quoted string containing parameters of the action, if any.

The %ACTION macro performs the following steps:

1. It checks whether the object was created.

2. It calls an appropriate method with corresponding parameters to perform the required action.

Each step is discussed using an example from the "Definition of Matrix Class" section of Chapter 2. For convenience, we will repeat the definition of the **mymatrix** object and all its elements.

The **mymatrix** object of the *Matrix* class and its components belonging to the *Vector* class are defined in the StatObj table:

StatObj table

STATOBJ	CLASS	ATTR_NO	ATTR_VAL
mymatrix	Matrix	1	column1
			column2
			column3
mymatrix	Matrix	2	20
column1	Vector	1	data1
column1	Vector	2	age
column2	Vector	1	data2
column2	Vector	2	weight
column3	Vector	1	data2
column3	Vector	2	height

The data objects that construct the defined statistical objects are defined in the Object and Property tables of the data dictionary tables:

Object table

OBJECT	DATASET	TITLE	LIBRARY
data1	demogrph	Demographic data about population	populatn
data2	medical	Medical data about population	populatn

Property table (selected columns)

OBJECT	COLUMN	TITLE	TYPE	LENGTH	ATTRIBUT
...	...	...	...	....	...
data1	AGE	Age	N	8	
data2	WEIGHT	Weight	N	8	
data2	HEIGHT	Height	N	8	

The main steps of the %ACTION macro program are as follows.

Step 1: Check whether the object was recently created

First, let's clarify what is meant by "an object is created." We have used this expression freely, but now is the time to consider its implementation.

As mentioned earlier, you can associate a data object or its specific columns to different statistical objects simultaneously. In this case, processing the different statistical objects may lead to changes in the data. Thus, we have to develop a mechanism to create and update statistical objects without damaging the source data object. Such a mechanism would perform the following steps:

1. Create a SAS library with reserved name _SA_WORK that serves as a work directory for creating statistical objects.

2. Add a new Status table to the Classes set of the data dictionary that contains information about the created statistical object.

3. Create in the _SA_WORK library a SAS data set with the same name as a statistical object and containing data copied from corresponding data objects.

The _SA_WORK SAS library is the place for storing and processing statistical objects. It creates several statistical objects based on the same data object, maintains source data, and can terminate or continue analysis from any point.

The Status table of the data dictionary contains the name of the created object and its class. Before performing an action on a statistical object, the %ACTION macro program checks the existence of this statistical object in the Status table.

The Status table is defined in the Object table of the Kernel set like this:

Object table

OBJECT	Dataset	Title	LIBRARY
Status	status	Created statistical objects	_sa_work

The Status table has only two columns that are defined in the Property table:

Property table (selected columns)

OBJECT	COLUMN	TITLE	TYPE	LENGTH	ATTRIBUT
...	...	...	...	....	...
Status	STATOBJ	Statistical object	C	8	P
Status	CLASS	Statistical class	C	20	P

In the example of the statistical object **mymatrix**, the %ACTION macro checks the existence of the object in the following ways:

1. It searches the Status table for the record containing "mymatrix" value in the STATOBJ column and "Matrix" value in the CLASS column.

2. If such a record was found, then %ACTION macro checks existence of the mymatrix data set in the _SA_WORK library.

3. If the record was not found in the Status table, and/or the data set was not found in the _SA_WORK library, the %ACTION macro interrupts its execution.

Step 2: Call an appropriate method with parameters

The %ACTION macro provides the correct call to an appropriate method for each specific object. At this step, the %ACTION macro evaluates data dictionary tables and obtains the necessary information about the statistical object, about the class that the object belongs to, and about the specific implementation of the action.

The %ACTION macro program also prepares parameters for the method. This means that, in addition to the parameters specified in the PARAMS column of the StatAct table or to those defined in the `params` parameter of the %ACTION macro, it adds the name of the statistical object as a first parameter for all methods.

For example, consider what the %ACTION macro program does if we submit the following code:

```
%action(object= mymatrix, action = "Extract", params=
"column1,= 0, drop");
```

The Extract action and its implementation for the *Matrix* class is described in "Preparing Data in Matrix" in Chapter 2. The %ACTION macro program performs the following steps:

1. It evaluates the StatObj data dictionary table to obtain the name of the class that the **mymatrix** object belongs to.

2. It evaluates the ClassMet table to obtain the name of the method implementing the "Extract" action for the *Matrix* class.

3. It calls the _mextr() method with "column1,= 0, drop" parameters, like this:

```
%_mextr(mymatrix,column1,= 0, drop);
```

The %_MEXTR macro program is given an additional parameter to those defined in the `params` parameter of the %ACTION macro. This additional parameter is the name of the statistical object, **mymatrix**, that all methods receive as their first parameter. This parameter also enables the %ACTION macro program to inform the method if the statistical object does not exist. There is a reserved word "NULL" that the %ACTION macro sends to the method as its first parameter when the statistical object is not found in the _SA_WORK library.

After discussing the functionality of the %ACTION macro program, we can start its implementation.

Implementation of the %ACTION macro program

The main technique that is implemented by the %ACTION macro program is the evaluation of the data dictionary tables. The following is the code of this macro program:

```
/*
 PROGRAM          ACTION
 DESCRIPTION      The macro implementing methods invocation
                  mechanism.
 USAGE            %action(object = object, action = action,
                  params = params);
 PARAMETERS
 REQUIRES         The &libref macro variable is a global macro
                  variable that contains the name of the SAS
                  library where the data dictionary tables are
                  located.
                  The &libwork macro variable is a global macro
                  variable that contains the name of the SAS
                  library where the created statistical objects
                  are located. In the book this library is
                  called _SA_WORK
 AUTHORS          T.Kolosova and S.Berestizhevsky.
*/
    %macro action(object = object, action = action, params =
    params);
          %let class = ;
          %let method = ;
          %let status = 0 ;
          %let dsexist = 0 ;
           %let action =  %substr(%bquote(&action), 2,
                          %eval(%length(&action)-2)) ;
          data _null_ ;
             set &libref..StatObj (where = (upcase(statobj)
             = upcase("&object"))) ;
             call symput("class", class) ;
          run ;

          data _null_ ;
             set &libref..ClassMet (where = (upcase(class)
             = upcase("&class") and
             upcase(action) = upcase("&action"))) ;
             call symput("method", method) ;
          run ;

          data _null_ ;
             set &libref..Status (where =
                (upcase(statobj) = upcase("&object") and
                 upcase(class) = upcase("&class"))) ;
             call symput("status", 1) ;
          run ;

          %if &status = 1 %then
          %do ;
             proc sql noprint;
                select count(*)
                into : dsexist from dictionary.members
                where   (libname ? upcase("&libwork"))
                      & (memname ? upcase("&object" ))
                      & (memtype ? "DATA");
             quit;

             %if &dsexist = 0 %then
                 %let object = NULL ;
          %end ;
          %if &status = 0 %then
             %let object = NULL ;

          %&method (&object, %substr(%bquote(&params), 2,
                   %eval(%length(&params)-2))) ;
     %mend ;
```

The Create Action and its implementation

The "Create Action" section in Chapter 2 introduces this generic action and defines it for each statistical class. Recall that an action is called generic if it exists for each class and differs only in its implementation.

The Create action has one input parameter:

`newobj` names the object that must be created.

The `newobj` parameter is given the name of the statistical object to be created.

Note: Each action is given the object name as its first parameter, in addition to those specified for the action. Hence, the Create action gets the object name twice. The %ACTION macro program replaces the object name with the "NULL" reserved word if the object does not exist. Two parameters of the Create action determine whether the object already exists and needs to be re-created, or whether it must be created for the first time.

Code for the macro programs implementing the Create action for different classes is available through the SAS Online Samples facility (for detailed information, refer to the inside back cover of the book). In this section we discuss common aspects of all implementations of the Create action, and consider an implementation of this action for the *Matrix* class only.

Creation of a statistical object consists of two steps:

1. Check correctness of the definition of the statistical object.

2. Create the object.

Step 1: Check correctness of the statistical object definition

To implement the first step, the Create action evaluates data dictionary tables. It searches for the name of the statistical object in the StatObj table of the data dictionary and checks its definition.

In the "Creating Matrices" section of Chapter 2 we defined the Create action for the *Matrix* class and specified the _mcreate() method that implements this action. Let's consider the %_MCREATE macro program as an example of an implementation of the Create action. In order to create the **mymatrix** object of the *Matrix* class, we submit the %ACTION macro program in the following way:

```
%action(object= mymatrix, action = "Create",
params="mymatrix");
```

This in turn submits the %_MCREATE macro program like this:

```
%_mcreate(mymatrix,mymatrix);
```

The *Matrix* class defines non-atomic statistical objects. In order to check the definition of the **mymatrix** object of the *Matrix* class, the %_MCREATE macro program does the following:

1. It finds the "mymatrix" value in the STATOBJ column of the StatObj table.

2. It reads attributes of the **mymatrix** object from the ATTR_NO and ATTR_VAL columns of the StatObj table.

3. It checks the first parameter of the object; it must be a list of objects of the *Vector* class, or an object of the *Vector Character* class, which in turn contains names of objects of the *Vector* class.

4. It checks the second parameter, which must either be a number or be omitted.

If the **mymatrix** object is defined correctly, its creation is started.

Step 2: Create the statistical object

Creation of statistical objects must be done recursively. For atomic statistical objects there is only one creation step because, by definition, atomic objects consist of data objects. For complex (non-atomic) objects, creation must continue down to an atomic object.

Creation of an object of the *Matrix* class is performed recursively, as it is a non-atomic class.

%_MCREATE macro program

The %_MCREATE macro program does the following:

1. It takes a list of the objects of the *Vector* class, either from the list of objects or from the object of the *Vector Character* class.

2. It creates these objects by submitting the %ACTION macro with a Create action for each of them.

3. It joins the created statistical objects into the new **mymatrix** object.

Following is the code of the %_MCREATE macro program:

```
/*
  PROGRAM         _MCREATE
  DESCRIPTION     Creation of matrix object
  USAGE           %_mcreate (object, newobj) ;
  PARAMETERS      object and newobj  -- both contain the name of
                  the object of the Matrix class that must be
                  created. If %_mcreate macro is invoked by the
                  %ACTION macro, the object parameter may
                  contain the "NULL" value (see explanation of
                  the parameters in the  "Create action" section
                  in chapter 4)
  REQUIRES        The &libref and &libwork are global macro
                  variables that contain the SAS library names
                  for data dictionary tables and for statistical
                  objects.
  AUTHORS         T.Kolosova and S.Berestizhevsky.
*/
   %macro _mcreate (object, newobj) ;
/*
  Checks correctness of definition of of the matrix object
*/

     %local aval1 aval2 ;
     %let attr_no = 0 ;
     %let aval1 = 0 ;
     %let aval2 = 0 ;
     %let exit = 0 ;
     %let vc_obj =  ;
/*
Gets the attributes of the object defined in the StatObj table
*/
```

```
       data _null_ ;
           retain i 0 ;
           set &libref..Statobj (where =
               (upcase(left(statobj)) =
                upcase(left("&newobj")))) ;
           call symput("attr_no", left(attr_no)) ;
           call symput("aval" || left(attr_no),
                         left(attr_val)) ;
           if attr_no > i+1 then
           do ;
               do j = i+1 to attr_no - 1 ;
                   call symput("aval" || left(j), " ");
               end;
           end ;
           i = attr_no ;
       run;
/*
  Analyzes the attributes
*/

       %let v_obj_no = 0 ;

       data _null_;
           length tmp $80;
           if symget("attr_no") < 1 or
               symget("attr_no") > 2 then
               link err_exit;
           if trim(symget("aval1")) = "" then
               link err_exit;
           tmp = scan(symget("aval1"), 1 , " ");
           if length(trim(tmp)) <
               length(trim(symget("aval1")))
           then do;
               i = 1;
               do while (trim(tmp) ^= "") ;
                   call symput("vobj" || left(i),
                                 left(trim(tmp)));
                   i+1;
                   tmp = scan(symget("aval1"), i ," ");
               end ;
               call symput("v_obj_no", left(i-1));
           end;
           else
           call symput("vc_obj",
               left(trim(symget("aval1")))) ;
           if symget("attr_no") = 2 then
           do;
               if trim(symget("aval2")) = "" then
                   call symput("aval2", 0) ;
           end ;
           return ;
       err_exit:
           call symput("exit",1) ;
           stop ;
       return ;
       run;

       %if &exit = 1 %then %goto err_exit ;
/*
  Analyzes the attributes' values
*/

       %if &vc_obj ^= %then
       %do ;
           data _null_;
               set &libref..Statobj (where =
           upcase(left(statobj)) = upcase(left("&vc_obj")));
```

```
            if upcase(left(class)) ^= "VECTOR CHARACTER" then
                    call symput("exit", 1);
          run ;
          %if &exit = 1 %then %goto err_exit;
   /*
   Call  the Get Elements action for the Vector Character object
          %action(object = &vc_obj, action = "Get Elements",
                  params =
                      "outobj, statobj");
   */

          data outobj ;
             set outobj ;
             statobj = left(upcase(statobj)) ;
          run;
       %end;
       %else
       %do;
          %if &v_obj_no < 2 %then %goto err_exit;

          data outobj;
             length statobj $8 ;
             %do i = 1 %to &v_obj_no;
                 statobj = left(upcase("&&vobj&i")) ;
                 output;
             %end;
          run;
       %end;
       proc sort data = &libref..statobj out = statobj
   (keep = statobj class)
   nodupkey;
   by statobj;
   run;

   data statobj;
       set statobj;
       statobj = left(upcase(statobj));
   run ;

   proc sort data = outobj;
   by statobj;
   run;

   data outobj(keep = statobj class);
       merge statobj (in = left) outobj (in=right);
       by statobj;
       if right;
   run ;

   %let v_obj_no = 0;
   data _null_;
       set outobj;
       retain v_obj_no 0;
       v_obj_no + 1;
       if upcase(left(class)) ^= "VECTOR" then
       do ;
           call symput("exit",1);
           stop;
       end;
       call symput("v_obj_no", left(v_obj_no));
       call symput("vobj" || left(v_obj_no), statobj);
   run;

     %if &exit = 1 or &v_obj_no = 0 %then %goto err_exit;
   /*
     Creates all vector objects
   */
```

```
      %do i = 1 %to &v_obj_no;
         %action(object = &&vobj&i, action = "Create",
                 params = "&&vobj&i");
      %end;
/*
  Creates the matrix object
*/

      data &libwork..&newobj ;
         %do i = 1 %to &v_obj_no;
            set &libwork..&&vobj&i ;
         %end;
         %if &aval2 > 0 %then
         %do;
            (obs = &aval2)
         %end;
         ;
      run;
/*
  Updates the Status table if an object with such a name exists
*/

      %if %upcase(&object) = %upcase(&newobj) %then
      %do;
         data &libref..status ;
            set &libref..status ;
            if upcase(left(statobj)) =
               upcase(left("&newobj")) then
               class = "Matrix";
         run;
      %end;
      %else %do ;
         data &libref..status ;
            set &libref..status (in = last);
            output;
            if _n_ = last then
            do;
               statobj = upcase(left("&newobj"))  ;
               class = "Matrix";
               output;
            end;
         run;
      %end ;

   %err_exit:
   %mend ;
```

%_VHIST macro program

The %_VHIST macro program implements the Histogram action for the *Vector* class. It calculates empirical distribution for an object of the *Vector* class, stores distribution in an object of the *Vector Distribution* class, and displays results in graphical form. This macro program gets the same parameters as they were defined for the Histogram action:

    `outobj`   name of the output object containing results

    `outdev`   name of the output device for the graphical presentation

The %_VHIST macro program does the following:

1. It sorts data of the statistical object and calculates the empirical distribution.

2. It creates an output object of the *Vector Distribution* class.

3. It creates a histogram and prints or displays it on the screen.

The code of this macro program is quite short, as shown here:

```
/*
   PROGRAM          _VHIST
   DESCRIPTION      Calculation of  empirical distribution and
                    creation of histogram for object of the Vector
                    class
   USAGE            %_vhist (object, outobj, outdev) ;
   PARAMETERS       object -the name of the statistical object of
                    the Vector class
                    outobj - the name of the statistical object of
                    the Vector Statistics class containing
                    calculated descriptive statistics
                    outdev - the name of the output device for
                    histogram. If outdev contains the name of the
                    file, then %_vhist macro will save the
                    produced histogram as picture in the GIF
                    format.
   REQUIRES         The &libwork is a global macro variable
                    defining the _SA_WORK library that contains
                    statistical objects
   AUTHORS          T.Kolosova and S.Berestizhevsky.
*/
%macro _vhist (object, outobj, outdev) ;

   %if %upcase(&object) = NULL %then
      %goto err_exit;

   %if &outdev ^= %then
   %do;
      %if %upcase(&outdev) ^= SCREEN %then
         filename outgif "&outdev" ; ;
      goptions reset=global
      norotate hpos=0 vpos=0
      %if %upcase(&outdev) ^= SCREEN %then
      %do ;
            device = imggif
            gsfname = outgif
            gsfmode = replace
            gsflen = 80
            gaccess = sasgastd
      %end ;
      cback= white
      ctext = black
      ftext=SWISSL
      interpol=join
      graphrc
      display ;

      pattern1 value=SOLID;
      axis1
         color=blue
         width=2.0 ;
      axis2
         color=blue
         width=2.0 ;
   %end ;
```

```
      proc capability data = &libwork..&object graphics
         %if &outobj ^= %then %do;
            noprint
         %end;
         ;
         var &object ;
         histogram &object /
         %if &outobj ^= %then %do;
            outhistogram = _out_
         %end;
         %if %upcase(&outdev) = %then %do;
            noplot
         %end;
         ;
      run ;

      %if &outobj ^= %then
      %do;

         data _null_;
            set &libwork..&object nobs = last;
            length min max 8 ;
            retain min max ;
            if _n_ = 1 then
            do;
               min = &object;
               max = &object;
            end;
            if min > &object then min = &object;
            if max < &object then max = &object;
            if _n_ = last then
            do ;
               call symput("min", min);
               call symput("max", max);
               call symput("obs", _n_);
            end ;
         run;

         data _out1_ (keep = left right value cumvalue
                      freq cumfreq);
            set _out1_;
            length left right value cumvalue freq cumfreq
                   delta 8;
            retain delta cumvalue cumfreq 0 ;
            if _n_ = 1 then
            do;
               delta = _midpt_ - min ;
            end;
            left = _midpt_ - delta ;
            right = _midpt_ + delta ;
            value = _obspct_ * &obs ;
            cumvalue + value ;
            freq = _obspct_;
            cumfreq + freq;
         run;
/*
 Creates and fills in the output object of the Vector
 Distribution class
*/
         %action(object = &outobj, action = "Create",
         params = "&outobj");
         %action(object = &outobj, action = "Put
         Elements", params = "_out1_, left, right, value,
         cumvalue, freq, cumfreq");
      %end ;
%err_exit:
%mend ;
```

%_VTRANS macro program

The %_VTRANS macro program applies a specific calculation to an object of the *Vector* class and stores the results in another object of the *Vector* class.

As the %_VTRANS macro program implements the Transform action for the *Vector* class, it has the same parameters as the action:

transform   transformation formula

outobj   name of the output object

A transformation that must be done on an object is defined in two ways:

- by keywords

- by an implicitly specified formula in SAS syntax.

Let's specify several keywords and their meanings:

LOG   logarithmic transformation

LOGN   log-normal transformation

INV   inverse

Each keyword refers to a specific transformation, and thus needs appropriate implementation. You can extend this list as needed, and then add implementation of the new transformation to the %_VTRANS macro program.

Implicit specification of a transformation formula is implemented once for all cases. The formula must be specified in SAS syntax and use the "#" symbol instead of a variable name. For example, the following formula answers these requirements and enables a quite complex transformation:

$1/(\cos(\#))^2$

Finally, the %_VTRANS macro program does the following:

1. It applies the specified transformation to the statistical object.

2. It stores the results in the output object of the *Vector* class.

The implementation of this program is very simple, and you can write it yourself. Our version of this program is available through the SAS Online Samples facility (for detailed information, refer to the inside back cover of the book).

%_MPLOT macro program

The %_MPLOT macro function implements the Scatter Plot action for the *Matrix* class. This macro produces a scatter plot of two variables and prints it or displays it on the screen. The %_MPLOT requires the following parameters:

`axisx`   name of the object element that is used for X axis

`axisy`   name of the object element that is used for Y axis

`outdev`   name of the output device

We consider here a very simple implementation of this action, that looks like this:

```
/*
PROGRAM          _MPLOT
DESCRIPTION      Creation of scatter plot for object of the
                 Matrix class
USAGE            %_mplot (object, axisx, axisy, outdev) ;
PARAMETERS       object - the name of the statistical object of
                 the Matrix class
                 axisx - the name of the object element that is
                 used for X axis
                 axisy - the name of the object element that is
                 used for Y axis
                 outdev - the name of the output device for
                 plot. If outdev contains the name of the file,
                 then %_mplot macro will save the produced plot
                 as picture in the GIF format.
REQUIRES         The &libwork is a global macro variable
                 defining the _SA_WORK library that contains
                 statistical objects
AUTHORS          T.Kolosova and S.Berestizhevsky.
*/
%macro _mplot (object, axisx, axisy, outdev) ;

    %if %upcase(&object) = NULL %then
        %goto err_exit ;

    %if %upcase(&outdev) ^= SCREEN %then
            filename outgif "&outdev" ; ;
    goptions reset=global
    norotate hpos=0 vpos=0
    %if %upcase(&outdev) ^= SCREEN %then
    %do ;
            device = imggif
            gsfname = outgif
            gsfmode = replace
            gsflen = 80
            gaccess = sasgastd
    %end ;
    cback = white
    ctext = black
    ftext = SWISSL
    interpol = none
    graphrc
    display ;

    pattern1 value = SOLID;
    axis1
        color=blue
        width=2.0 ;
    axis2
        color=blue
```

```
       width=2.0 ;
symbol1 c = blue
    i = none
    l = 1
    v = STAR
    cv = blue ;

proc gplot data= &libwork..&object ;
    plot &axisy * &axisx /
        haxis=axis1
        vaxis=axis2
        frame ;
run;
quit;

%err_exit :
%mend ;
```

You can add, if you want, more parameters to the Scatter Plot action that will control the appearance of the plot, for example, colors of lines, background, title, and so on.

%_MODEL macro program

The %_MODEL macro program implements the Model action that performs fitting of a model to experimental data. The %_MODEL macro program requires the following parameters:

model   names the dependent and independent variables

outobj   name of the object that contains results of the "Model" action

The model parameter specifies a model to be fit.

The outobj parameter specifies an output object containing the results.

The %_MODEL macro program does the following:

1. It fits linear regression models by least-squares. This step is written using PROC REG. We used a set of fairly general PROC REG options. However, you can add more parameters to the Model action to control which statistics are calculated and by which method.

2. It creates an output object that contains parameter estimates, optional statistics, and diagnostic measures calculated after fitting the model.

The following is the code for the %_MODEL macro program:

```
/*
  PROGRAM          _MODEL
  DESCRIPTION      Fitting of a model to experimental data
  USAGE            %_model (object, model, outobj) ;
  PARAMETERS       object - the name of the statistical object of
                   the Model class
                   model - the model to be fitted
                   outobj - the name of the object of the List
                   class containing the results of the model
                   fitting
  REQUIRES         The &libwork is a global macro variable
                   defining the _SA_WORK library that contains
                   statistical objects
  AUTHORS          T.Kolosova and S.Berestizhevsky.
*/
  %macro _model(object, model, outobj);

    %if %upcase(&object) = NULL %then
         %goto err_exit ;

    %let model =
    %substr(%bquote(&model),2,%eval(%length(&model)-2)) ;

       proc reg data = &libwork.&object
          %if &outobj ^= %then %do;
             outest = _stat_ noprint
          %end;
          ;
          model &model ;
          %if &outobj ^= %then %do;
             output out = _out_
             P=P
             R=R
             L95M=L95M
             U95M=U95M
             L95=L95
             U95=U95
             STDP=STDP
             STDR=STDR
             STDI=STDI
             STUDENT=STUDENT
             COOKD=COOKD
             H=H
             PRESS=PRESS
             RSTUDENT=RSTUDENT
             DFFITS=DFFITS
             COVRATIO=COVRATIO;
          %end;
       run;
       quit;

       %if &outobj ^= %then %do;
          %let actual = %scan(&model,1,=);

          data _out_;
             set _out_ (keep = &actual
                P R L95M U95M L95 U95 STDP STDR STDI STUDENT
                COOKD H PRESS RSTUDENT DFFITS COVRATIO
                rename = (&actual = actual));
             if actual ^= .;
          run;
```

```
      proc transpose data = _stat_
      (drop = _model_ _type_ _depvar_ intercep &actual)
      out = _stat1_ (rename = (col1 = statval _name_ =
      statname) drop = _label_);
      run;

      %action(object = &outobj,action="Put Elements",
                    params="_stat1_,_out_");
   %end;
   %err_exit:
%mend;
```

%_FITPLOT macro program

The %_FITPLOT macro program implements the Fit Plot action for the *Model Statistics* class. The parameters of the %_FITPLOT macro program are the same as the parameters in the Fit Plot action:

axisx   names the object element that is used for X axis

axisy   names the object elements that are used for Y axis

outdev   name of the output device

The implementation of the Fit Plot action is very similar to that of the Scatter Plot action, so you can use the %_MPLOT macro program as an example for writing the %_FITPLOT macro. Hevower, the differences between these two actions and their implementations are as follows:

- The %_FITPLOT permits multivariable plot.

- The %_FITPLOT is based on the *Model Statistics* class, which assigns a special statistical meaning to each element.

You may wish to develop your own version of the %_FITPLOT macro program. Our implementation is available through the SAS Online Samples facility (for detailed information, refer to the inside back cover of the book).

Example for the Data Analyst

This example is intended for the data analyst. Here we want to show how to use the defined classes to perform object-oriented statistical analysis. The main goal of this example is not to show how to solve the specific problem, but how to use the object-oriented approach to statistical programming and analysis for correct, iterative solving of any data analysis problem.

Let's return to the specific analysis problem that we started with: we want to analyze data stored in the Cars data object and to model the effect that weight has on the gas mileage of a car. Consider the required steps to get results (some of these steps have already been described in previous chapters).

Step 1: Define the data object

First, you have to define the data object to be analyzed. This was done in Chapter 1. The definition of the Cars object is shown here:

Object table

OBJECT	DATASET	TITLE	LIBRARY
cars	cars	Automobile Data Table	automob

Property table (selected columns)

OBJECT	COLUMN	TITLE	TYPE	LENGTH	ATTRIBUT
...	...	...	...	....	...
cars	COUNTRY	Country	C	20	P
cars	TYPE	Type of a car	C	10	P
cars	RELIABIL	Reliability mark	N	8	
cars	MILEAGE	Mileage data	N	8	
cars	WEIGHT	Weight of a car	N	8	

Step 2: Define the statistical object

In this step you associate the data object with an appropriate statistical class to define a new statistical object.

Let's define the **mil2weit** object of the *Model* class.

Recall that an object of the *Model* class is defined by specifying the object of the *Matrix* class, which contains data for analysis.

The definition of this new statistical object in the StatObj table looks like this:

StatObj table

STATOBJ	CLASS	ATTR_NO	ATTR_VAL
mil2weit	Model	1	milweitm

This definition means that there must be a **milweitm** object of the *Matrix* class. Let's define this object in the StatObj table:

StatObj table

STATOBJ	CLASS	ATTR_NO	ATTR_VAL
milweitm	Matrix	1	mileage weight
mileage	Vector	1	cars
mileage	Vector	2	mileage
weight	Vector	1	cars
weight	Vector	2	weight

As the StatObj table shows, the **milweitm** object of the *Matrix* class has two elements: **mileage** and **weight**. The **mileage** object of the *Vector* class is defined on the MILEAGE column of the Cars data object, and the **weight** object of the *Vector* class is based on the WEIGHT column of the Cars data object.

This completes the definition of the **mil2weit** statistical object of the *Model* class, and we can now start analyzing its data.

Step 3: Study the graphics of the data

We start the analysis by viewing each variable separately.

First, look at the univariate characteristics of the data. You perform the Descriptive action on the **mileage** and **weight** objects of the *Vector* class by submitting the following:

```
%action(object=mileage, action="Descriptive");

%action(object=weight, action="Descriptive");
```

These actions produce the following results for MILEAGE and WEIGHT, respectively:

```
                       Analysis Variable : MILEAGE


   N  Nmiss    Minimum     Maximum      Range        Sum
  ------------------------------------------------------------------
  53   58     18.0000000  37.0000000  19.0000000   1327.00
  ------------------------------------------------------------------


        Mean       Variance     Std Dev     Std Error       CV
  ------------------------------------------------------------------
    25.0377358   24.0370102   4.9027554   0.6734452   19.5814645
  ------------------------------------------------------------------


             Skewness    Kurtosis
           ----------------------------------------
            0.6153304   -0.3751260
           ----------------------------------------
```

Analysis Variable : WEIGHT				
N	Nmiss	Minimum	Maximum	Range	Sum
108	3	1695.00	4285.00	2590.00	319315.00

Mean	Variance	Std Dev	Std Error	CV
2956.62	302921.42	550.3829715	52.9606261	18.6152736

Skewness	Kurtosis
0.0988142	-0.5892075

You can also see distribution of each variable using the Histogram action. Submit the following:

```
%action(object=mileage, action="Histogram",
params=",screen");

%action(object=weight, action="Histogram",
params=",screen");
```

to get the following results:

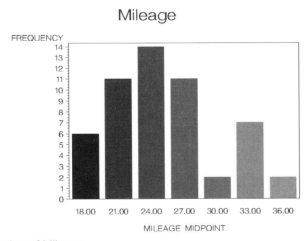

Figure 4.1 Distribution of Mileage

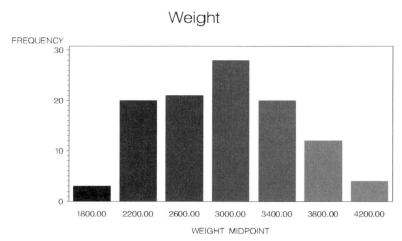

Figure 4.2 Distribution of Weight

Step 4: Reveal low-dimensional relationships

By creating a scatter plot of mileage (miles per gallon) of all cars versus their weights, you can examine the relationships between these variables. Submit the following:

```
%action(object=milweitm, action="Scatter Plot",
params="mileage, weight, screen");
```

The output is as follows:

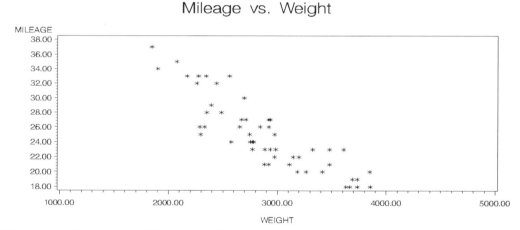

Figure 4.3 Scatter plot of Mileage vs. Weight

This scatter plot displays a curved relationship among the data. This might suggest a non-linear relationship. To get linear relationships, you can try some transformations of variables. Linear models are relatively easy to fit, and they have well-understood statistical properties.

Step 5: Transform data

We initially plotted mileage (miles per gallon) of a car versus its weight. Let's try the inverse of the mileage variable and get gallons per mile. We store the results of these transformations in the new **galonmil** object of the *Vector* class, which is defined like this:

StatObj table

STATOBJ	CLASS	ATTR_NO	ATTR_VAL
galonmil	Vector	1	cars
galonmil	Vector	2	galonmil

We also add a new column to the Cars data object:

Property table (selected columns)

OBJECT	COLUMN	TITLE	TYPE	LENGTH	ATTRIBUT
...	...	...	...	....	...
cars	COUNTRY	Country	C	20	P
cars	TYPE	Type of a car	C	10	P
cars	RELIABIL	Reliability mark	N	8	
cars	MILEAGE	Mileage data	N	8	
cars	WEIGHT	Weight of a car	N	8	
cars	GALONMIL	Gallons per mile	N	8	

Submit the following:

```
%action(object=mileage, action="Transform",
params="inv, galonmil");
```

As a result of this action, the inversed mileage variable is stored in the **galonmil** object of the *Vector* class.

Step 6: Choose a model

Before creating a new scatter plot, add a new definition to the StatObj table:

StatObj table

STATOBJ	CLASS	ATTR_NO	ATTR_VAL
milweitm	Matrix	1	mileage weight galonmil

The only required change is the number of elements composing the **milweitm** object. Now it contains an additional **galonmil** element.

To get a scatter plot, you submit the following macro:

```
%action(object=milweitm, action="Scatter Plot",
params="galonmil,weight,screen");
```

The output that you get is as follows:

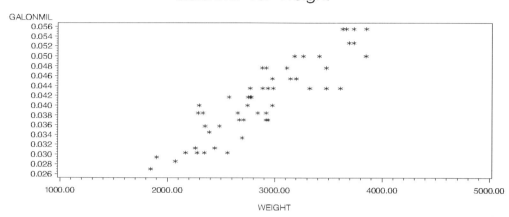

Figure 4.4   Scatter plot of Galonmil vs. Weight

The gallons per mile appear to be more linear with respect to weight, so we expect a good fit using a linear model. This formula defines the model:

galonmil ~ weight

After we have selected the model, we can fit it.

Step 7: Fit the model

To fit the model, you just use the Model action of the *Model* class.

If you want to store the results of the Model action permanently for further analysis, you have to define an output object of the *List* class that in turn contains one object of the *Table Statistics* class, and an object of the *Model Statistics* class. Let's call this object **milweitr**, its first element (of the *Table Statistics* class) - **mw_table**, and its second element (of the *Model Statistics* class) - **mw_model**. We suggest you define this object yourself, using an example of definition of the **anovares** object in "Example of Designing a New Class and Its Methods" in Chapter 3.

You submit the Model action for the **mil2weit** object like this:

```
%action(object=mil2weit, action="Model", params=
"'galonmil=weight',milweitr");
```

Step 8: Examine the fit

To examine the fit, plot the regression line using the Fit Plot action of the *Model Statistics* class. Suppose that you want to see two plots with the following values:

- actual and predicted values with the upper and lower 95% confidence interval for an individual prediction

- residuals vs. actual values.

Submit the following macro programs:

```
%action(object=mw_model, action="Fit Plot",
params=",actual predicted u95 l95, screen");

%action(object=mw_model, action="Fit Plot",
params="actual ,residual, screen");
```

These produce the following plots:

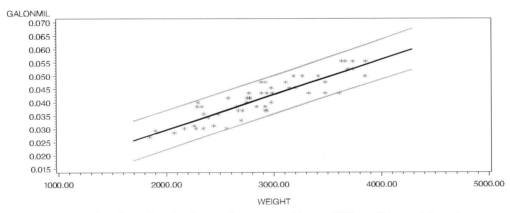

Figure 4.5 Actual and predicted values with upper and lower 95% confidence interval

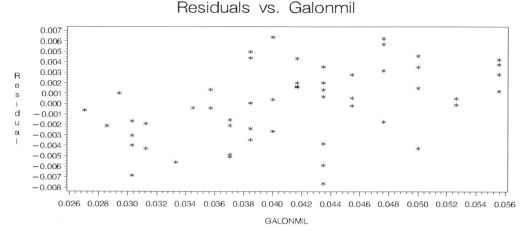

Figure 4.6   Residuals vs. actual values

Residuals that are scattered with no pattern suggest that the model fits the data.

Step 9: Creating the procedure

As a data analyst, you often have to repeat the same analysis process for new data. Such a process can be automated by defining the actions in the StatAct table. For this example, you define the following analysis procedure:

StatAct table

ANALYSID	ORDER	STATOBJ	ACTION	PARAMS
mw_ex	1	mileage	DESCRIPTIVE	
mw_ex	2	weight	DESCRIPTIVE	
mw_ex	3	mileage	HISTOGRAM	,screen
mw_ex	4	weight	HISTOGRAM	,screen
mw_ex	5	mileage	TRANSFORM	inv, galonmil
mw_ex	6	milweitm	SCATTER PLOT	galonmil, weight, screen
mw_ex	7	mil2weit	MODEL	'galonmil =weight', milweitr
mw_ex	8	mw_model	FIT PLOT	,actual predicted u95m l95m, screen
mw_ex	9	mw_model	FIT PLOT	actual, residual, screen

For example, each time that the Cars data object is updated with new data, you have to submit only one line of code:

```
%analyze(mw_ex);
```

Summary

The goal of this chapter was to give you tools and examples that will enable you to design your own statistical classes and methods, and to create flexible and correct analyzing tools. The next chapter gives you one more example of how to use the object-oriented approach to statistical programming and analysis.

CHAPTER 5

Example: Object-Oriented Time Series Analysis

Introduction

A time series is used in situations where the timing of the data acquisition is an important feature of the values and their analysis.

This chapter describes how to create, visualize, and process time series in SAS using an object-oriented approach to statistical programming and analysis. We consider the following steps in using this approach:

1. Define data objects and appropriate statistical classes.

2. Define permitted actions and the peculiarities of their implementation for each class.

3. Implement these actions as macro functions that evaluate tables of the data dictionary.

4. Use created statistical classes for analysis of time series.

The object-oriented approach to statistical analysis of a time series insures that the time series will be analyzed correctly by methods that allow correct interpretation of results.

Definition of Time Series Classes

A time series is a collection of observations that are made sequentially. We recognize three kinds of time series:

- regularly spaced time series, that is, a sequence of observations obtained at equal intervals

- calendar time series, in which regularly spaced observations are associated with calendar dates

- irregularly spaced time series, in which observations may be sampled at irregular intervals.

A time series can be either univariate or multivariate. In the first case it can be represented as a vector or a factor, while in the second case it can be represented as a matrix or a data table.

Regular Time Series

A regular time series is characterized by three time parameters that provide a summary of the sequence of observation times, namely:

- the time of the first observation

- either the interval between observation times or the sampling rate (frequency)

- the time of the last observation.

Any data that is measured at regular time intervals can be represented as objects of the *Regular Time Series* class.

Class Definition

The new *Regular Time Series* class is intended to store and manipulate statistical objects that conform to the definition of the regular time series. The definition of the *Regular Time Series* class in the Class table looks like this:

Class table

CLASS	SPRCLASS	DESCRIPT
Regular Time Series	Main	Regularly spaced time series

Attributes

This class has six attributes that specify the name of the data object where the observations are stored, time parameters described above, and units of the observation interval. These attributes are defined in the ClassAtr table like this:

ClassAtr table

CLASS	ATTR_NO	ATTRNAME	ATTRDESC
Regular Time Series	1	OBJECT	Name of the data object that stores time series observations
Regular Time Series	2	FIRST	The time of the first observation
Regular Time Series	3	LAST	The time of the last observation
Regular Time Series	4	DELTA	The interval between observation times
Regular Time Series	5	FREQ	The sampling rate – the number of observations per sampling period – which is the reciprocal of the interval between observation times.
Regular Time Series	6	UNITS	The units of the observation interval

The OBJECT attribute of the *Regular Time* Series class stores a name of an object that must belong to one of the following classes: the *Vector*, *Vector Discrete*, *Matrix*, *Factor*, or *Data Table*.

The FIRST and LAST attributes contain the time of the first and the last observations respectively.

The DELTA and FREQ attributes are reciprocals: you can define either one, and the other can be calculated. For example, suppose you want to make a time series of the outcomes of presidential elections, which are held every four years. In this case it is easier to define the DELTA attribute. But when the observation intervals occur more frequently, it is often easier to define the FREQ attribute.

The UNITS attribute defines measurement units of the interval between observations.

Let's consider an example definition of two objects of the *Regular Time Series* class. The **election** object stores data about outcomes of presidential elections, and the **cycle** object stores electricity production data. The definitions of these objects in the StatObj tables look like this:

StatObj table

STATOBJ	CLASS	ATTR_NO	ATTR_VAL
election	Regular Time Series	1	votes
election	Regular Time Series	2	1856
election	Regular Time Series	3	1996
election	Regular Time Series	4	4
election	Regular Time Series	6	years
cycle	Regular Time Series	1	watts
cycle	Regular Time Series	2	1972
cycle	Regular Time Series	3	1989
cycle	Regular Time Series	5	12
cycle	Regular Time Series	6	years

As the StatObj table shows:

- the **election** object of the *Regular Time Series* class contains the **votes** object (ignore its class, for now), which consists of observations measured every 4 years from 1856 to 1996

- the **cycle** object of the *Regular Time Series* class contains the **watts** object, which contains monthly measurements from 1972 to 1989.

Calendar Time Series

A calendar time series is a sequence of observations, taken at regular intervals, in which each observation is associated with a calendar date. It means that time intervals are measured in days, weeks, years, and so on.

Class Definition

The *Calendar Time Series* class is intended to store and manipulate calendar time series. The definition of a calendar time series is very similar to that of the regular time series, so the *Calendar Time Series* class can be defined as a subclass of the *Regular Time Series* class:

Class table

CLASS	SPRCLASS	DESCRIPT
Calendar Time Series	Regular Time Series	Regularly spaced time series associated with calendar date

Attributes

According to the subclass/superclass relations, the *Calendar Time Series* class inherits its attributes from the *Regular Time Series* class. However, the UNITS attribute has an additional restriction: it can accept only one of the following values: "days", "weeks", "months", "quarters", or "years". Each of these units has a default sampling frequency, such as :

UNITS	FREQUENCY
"days"	365
"weeks"	52
"months"	12
"quarters"	4
"years"	1

In addition to the attributes that the *Calendar Time Series* class inherits from the *Regular Time Series* class, it has one more attribute:

ClassAtr table

CLASS	ATTR_NO	ATTRNAME	ATTRDESC
Calendar Time Series	1	MUNITS	Multiplier of the units of the observation interval

The MUNITS attribute works as a multiplier for the UNITS. Consider the following example: sometimes you have data that are obtained at regular intervals that are not one of the five units shown in the earlier table, for instance every ten days. The multiplier, set by the MUNITS attribute, allows intervals that are whole numbers of values of the UNITS attribute. So, to specify observations taken every ten days, set the value of the UNITS attribute to "days" and the value of the MUNITS attribute to 10. To specify semi-annual data, set the value of UNITS attribute to "months" and the value of the MUNITS attribute to 6. Any other intervals can be defined similarly.

Irregular Time Series

An irregular time series is a set of observations taken over time at unequal intervals. Each observation of an irregular time series is associated with an observation time. This class differs from the previous time series classes.

Class Definition

Let's define the *Irregular Time Series* class in the Class table:

Class table

CLASS	SPRCLASS	DESCRIPT
Irregular Time Series	Main	Class of irregularly spaced time series objects

Attributes

The *Irregular Time Series* class has three attributes: the name of the data object that stores observations, the vector containing the times of each successive observation, and the units in which the observation time is measured. The definition of attributes of the *Irregular Time Series* class looks like this:

ClassAtr table

CLASS	ATTR_NO	ATTRNAME	ATTRDESC
Irregular Time Series	1	OBJECT	Name of the data object that stores observations
Irregular Time Series	2	TIMEVEC	The vector containing the times of each successive observation
Irregular Time Series	3	UNITS	The units by which the observation time is measured

The OBJECT attribute of the *Irregular Time* Series class stores the name of an object that must belong to one of the following classes: *Vector*, *Vector Discrete*, *Matrix*, *Factor*, or *Data Table*.

The values of the TIMEVEC attribute may get the name of the object belonging either to the *Vector Numeric* class or the *Vector Character* class. In the second case, the object must contain dates in ascending order. Of course, the objects of the *Irregular Time Series* class can be created, plotted, or summarized in the same way as objects of the *Regular Time Series* class.

Definition of Actions

In the previous section we have defined three new classes for time series; now we will discuss their actions.

We can define at least one generic action for the *Regular Time Series*, *Calendar Time Series* and *Irregular Time Series* classes – this is the Create action. The methods that implement this action are defined in the ClassMet table like this:

ClassMet table

CLASS	ACTION	METHOD	ACTDESC
Regular Time Series	CREATE	_rtcreat()	Creates an object of the Regular Time Series class
Calendar Time Series	CREATE	_ctcreat()	Creates an object of the Calendar Time Series class
Irregular Time Series	CREATE	_itcreat()	Creates an object of the Irregular Time Series class

In the section entitled "Example for the Programmer" in Chapter 4, we have already discussed in detail the Create action and its implementations. The implementations of the _rtcreat(), _ctcreat(), and _itcreat() methods are available through the SAS Online Samples facility (for detailed information, refer to the inside back cover of the book).

In the next section we consider actions that are specific for time series.

Box-Jenkins Strategy

The actions for time series closely follow the Box-Jenkins strategy for time series modeling, with features for the identification, the estimation and diagnostic checking, and the forecasting steps of the Box-Jenkins method[1].

1. To identify a time series, we create actions that compute autocorrelations, inverse autocorrelations, partial correlations, and cross correlations. The analysis of the results of these actions suggest one or several models that could be fit.

2. To estimate a model and calculate diagnostic statistics, we create an action that fits the model specified on the previous step, estimates the parameters of that model, and calculates diagnostic statistics. These statistics help judge the adequacy of the model. If the diagnostic statistics indicate problems with the model, we try another model and repeat the estimation and diagnostic checking action.

3. For forecasting future values of a time series, we should create an action that predicts values of the time series and generates confidence intervals for them.

Next we consider actions for identification of time series, for model estimation, and for generating diagnostic statistics.

---

[1] Box, G.E.P. and Jenkins, G.M., *Time Series Analysis: Forecasting and Control*, San Francisco: Holden-Day, 1976

Actions for Identification

Time series data is collected over time, so there may be a correlation between successive observations. You can visually explore whether or not the data is serially correlated by using actions producing the following kinds of plots:

- simple time series plots

- lagged scatter plots

- autocorrelation function plots.

To illustrate use of the actions, we used real time series data, which is partially presented in the following table:

Travels

Date	International Airline Travel (Thousands)
01JAN49	112
01FEB49	118
01MAR49	132
01APR49	129
01MAY49	121
01AUG56	405
...	...
...	...
01SEP56	355
01FEB58	318
01MAR58	362
01APR58	348
01MAY58	363
01JUN58	435
01JUL58	491
01AUG58	505
01SEP58	404
01OCT58	359
01NOV58	310
01DEC58	337
01JAN59	360
01FEB59	342
01MAR59	406
01APR59	396
01AUG60	606
01SEP60	508
01OCT60	461
01NOV60	390
01DEC60	432

All data is located in the SASHELP.AIR data set, which is provided in the SAS System. Let's define the Travel data object in the Object and Property data dictionary tables like this:

Object table

OBJECT	DATASET	TITLE	LIBRARY
travel	air	International airline travel data	sashelp

Property table (selected columns)

OBJECT	COLUMN	TITLE	TYPE	LENGTH
...	...	...	...	....
travel	DATE	Observation date	N	8
travel	AIR	Number of air travels	N	8

We define the **travel** statistical object of the *Calendar Time Series* class in the StatObj data dictionary table:

StatObj table

STATOBJ	CLASS	ATTR_NO	ATTR_VAL
travel	Calendar Time Series	1	air
travel	Calendar Time Series	2	01JAN49
travel	Calendar Time Series	3	01DEC60
travel	Calendar Time Series	4	1
travel	Calendar Time Series	6	month
travel	Calendar Time Series	7	1
air	Vector	1	travel
air	Vector	2	air

You can interpret this definition like this:

- The **travel** statistical object of the *Calendar Time Series* class consists of the **air** object of the *Vector* class.

- The **travel** object contains monthly time series observations from January 1, 1949, to December 1, 1960.

- The **air** object of the *Vector* class is based on the AIR column of the **travel** data object.

Simple time series plots

The simple time series plot shows each observation plotted against its observation time.

Plot Action

The Plot action produces the plot of the data to the specified output device. This action can be defined for each time series class. The parameters of this action are

`elements`   names the object elements that are used for Y axis

`outdev`   name of the output device

As each time series class defines implicitly the observation time for each observation, the Plot action always knows what should be used for the X axis.

Because time series classes define either univariate or multivariate time series, the `elements` parameter can contain a single element or a list of elements for Y axis that will be plotted on one figure. This parameter can also be omitted, in which case the Plot action displays simple time series plots for each element of the class, one by one.

The `outdev` parameter specifies an output device – printer or screen.

The definition of the Plot action in the ClassMet table looks like this:

ClassMet table

CLASS	ACTION	METHOD	ACTDESC
Regular Time Series	PLOT	_rtplot()	Plots data of an object of the Regular Time Series class
Calendar Time Series	PLOT	_ctplot()	Plots data of an object of the Calendar Time Series class
Irregular Time Series	PLOT	_itplot()	Plots data of an object of the Irregular Time Series class

The implementations of the _rtplot(), _ctplot(), and _itplot() methods are available through the SAS Online Samples facility (for detailed information, refer to the inside back cover of the book).

For example, our time series presenting with the **travel** object of the *Calendar Time Series* class can be plotted as follows:

```
%action(object=travel, action="Plot", params = "air,
screen");
```

This action produces this plot:

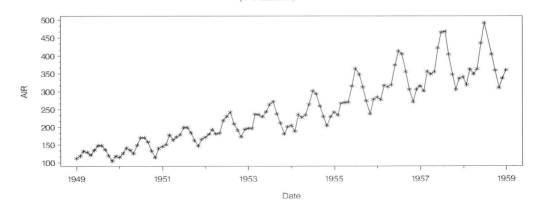

Figure 5.1 Simple time series plot

Lagged scatter plots

The values of successive observations in Figure 5.1 tend to be close together, so you suspect some serial correlation. There is a special action that enables you to see serial correlation more clearly.

Lags Action

The Lags action produces lagged scatter plots for objects of time series classes. The parameters of this action are similar to those of the Plot action:

element   name of the object element that is used for Y axis

outdev   name of the output device

The difference here is that the `element` parameter can contain only a single element for Y axis, but not a list of elements.

The `outdev` parameter specifies an output device – file or screen.

The definition of the Lags action in the ClassMet table looks like this:

ClassMet table

CLASS	ACTION	METHOD	ACTDESC
Regular Time Series	LAGS	_rtlags()	Produces lagged scatter plot of an object of the Regular Time Series class
Calendar Time Series	LAGS	_ctlags()	Produces lagged scatter plot of an object of the Calendar Time Series class
Irregular Time Series	LAGS	_itlags()	Produces lagged scatter plot of an object of the Irregular Time Series class

The implementation of the Lags action for time series classes is worth discussing. You can use different lag values to build lagged scatter plots. However, it is almost always enough to analyze up to lag equal 4. We propose to implement the Lags action in such a way that you get at once scatter plots of pairs of values of a time series separated by 1, 2, 3, and 4 time units.

The Lags action does the following:

1. It creates four lagged time series.

2. It produces lagged scatter plots with lag of 1, 2, 3, 4, ...

3. It displays four plots at the output device.

This is the code of the %_RTLAGS macro program that implements the Lags action for the *Regular Time Series* class:

```
/*
  PROGRAM         _RTLAGS
  DESCRIPTION     Producing of lagged scatter plots of an object
                  of the Regular Time Series class
  USAGE           %_rtlags (object, element, outdev) ;
  PARAMETERS      object - the name of the statistical object of
                  the Regular Time Series class
                  element - the name of the column of the
                  statistical object
                  outdev - the name of the output device for
                  plot. If outdev contains the name of the file,
                  then %_rtlags macro will save the produced
                  plot as picture in the GIF format.
  REQUIRES        The &libwork is a global macro variable
                  defining the _SA_WORK library that contains
                  statistical objects
  AUTHORS         T.Kolosova and S.Berestizhevsky.
*/
 %macro _rtlags (object, element, outdev) ;

    %if %upcase(&object) = NULL %then
       %goto err_exit ;
    %let lagsnum = 4 ;
    proc catalog c = work.gseg kill ;
    run ;
    quit ;

    %if %upcase(&outdev) ^= SCREEN %then
         filename outgif "&outdev" ; ;

    goptions reset=global
    norotate hpos=0 vpos=0
    %if %upcase(&outdev) ^= SCREEN %then
    %do ;
         device = imggif
         gsfname = outgif
         gsfmode = replace
         gsflen = 80
         gaccess = sasgastd
    %end ;
    cback = white
    ctext = black
    ftext = SWISSL
    interpol = none
    graphrc
    display ;

    pattern1 value = SOLID;
    axis1
       color=blue
       width=2.0 ;
    axis2
       color=blue
       width=2.0 ;

    symbol1 c = blue
    i = none
    l = 1
    v = STAR
    cv = blue ;
```

```
%do i = 1 %to &lagsnum ;
    %let dsid=%sysfunc(open(&libwork..&object,i));
    %if &dsid %then
    %do;
        %let len=%sysfunc(varlen(&dsid,
                %sysfunc(varnum(&dsid,&element))));
        %let rc=%sysfunc(close(&dsid));
    %end;

    data lag&i ;
        set &libwork..&object ;
        length lag&i &len ;
        lag&i = lag&i(&element) ;
    run ;

    title2 "Lagged Scatterplots: Lag = &i" ;

    proc gplot data= lag&i ;
    plot &element * lag&i /
    haxis=axis1
    vaxis=axis2
    frame ;
    run;
    quit;
%end ;

%do i = 1 %to &lagsnum ;
    data _null_;
        length grnum 8 ;
        grnum = symget('lagsnum');
        if grnum = 1 then do;
            call symput("_xl1",left(0));
            call symput("_xr1",left(100));
            call symput("_yl1",left(0));
            call symput("_yu1",left(100));
            return;
        end;
        if mod(grnum, 2) > 0 then
            grnum + 1 ;
        stop = 0;
        cols = 1;
        lines = grnum;
        do until(stop);
            c = cols * 2;
            if (floor(grnum/c))*c ^= grnum then
            do;
                stop = 1;
                lines = grnum/cols ;
            end;
            else do;
                l = grnum/c;
                if (c > 1) then
                    stop = 1;
                else do;
                    cols = c;
                    lines = l;
                end;
            end;
        end;
        width = 100/cols;
        height = 100/lines;
        c = 0 ;
        do i = 1 to lines;
            do j = 1 to cols;
                c + 1 ;
    call symput("_xl"||left(c),left((j-1) * width));
    call symput("_xr"||left(c),left(j * width));
    call symput("_yl"||left(c),left((i-1) * height));
```

```
         call symput("_yu"||left(c),left(i * height));
            end ;
         end;
      run;

      proc greplay tc = work.gseg nofs
         igout= work.gseg ;
         tdef tempspc
      %do k = 1 %to &lagsnum;
         &k/
         llx=&&_xl&k lly=&&_yl&k
         ulx=&&_xl&k uly=&&_yu&k
         urx=&&_xr&k ury=&&_yu&k
         lrx=&&_xr&k lry=&&_yl&k
      %end; ;

         template tempspc ;
         treplay
           1:gplot
      %do i=2 %to &lagsnum ;
         %let k = %eval(&i - 1);
         %if &k < 10 %then
         %do ;
              &i:gplot&k
         %end ;
         %else %do;
              &i:gplot&k
         %end;
      %end ; ;
      run;
      quit ;
   %end;

   %err_exit :
%mend ;
```

The implementations of the _ctlags() and _itlags() methods are available through the SAS Online Samples facility (for detailed information, refer to the inside back cover of the book).

For example, if you submit the following macro program, you can see clearly that the time series presenting by the **travel** object has a serial correlation:

```
%action(object=travel, action="Lags", params = "air,
screen");
```

The lagged scatter plots in the following figure plot pairs of values of a time series separated by 1, 2, 3, and 4 time units.

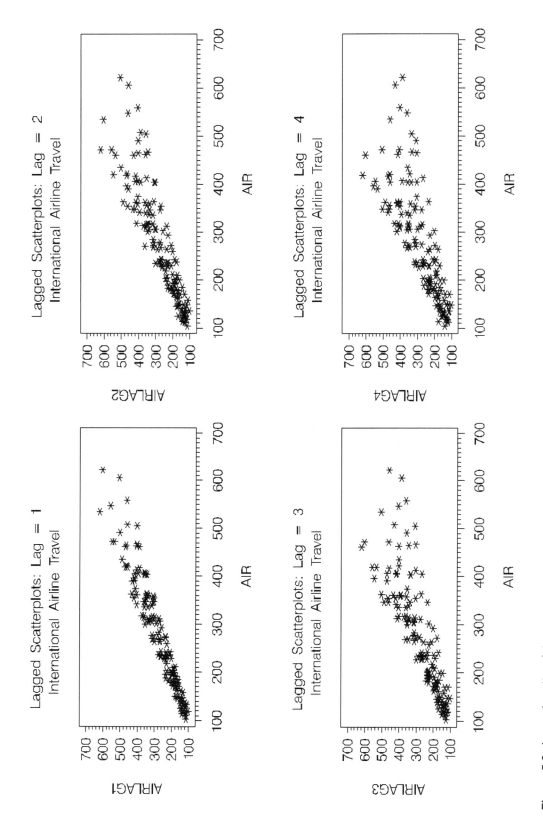

Figure 5.2 Lagged scatter plots

In this example, the airlag1 and airlag2 plots show evidence of a strong positive correlation, and the airlag3 and airlag4 plots indicate a less strong positive correlation.

Autocorrelation function plots

An autocorrelation function plot provides an estimation of the correlation between observations separated by a lag of 1,2,3, ...,*n* time units.

Autocorrelation Action

The Autocorrelation action produces autocorrelation function plots for objects of time series classes. The Autocorrelation action has the following parameter:

> `element`   names the object element

The `element` parameter gets a single element for the Y axis. The definition of the Autocorrelation action in the ClassMet table looks like this:

ClassMet table

CLASS	ACTION	METHOD	ACTDESC
Regular Time Series	AUTOCORRELATION	_rtauto()	Produces autocorrelation function plot of an object of the Regular Time Series class
Calendar Time Series	AUTOCORRELATION	_ctauto()	Produces autocorrelation function plot of an object of the Calendar Time Series class
Irregular Time Series	AUTOCORRELATION	_itauto()	Produces autocorrelation function plot of an object of the Irregular Time Series class

To implement the Autocorrelation action we used the ARIMA procedure.

This is the code of the %_RTAUTO macro program that implements the Autocorrelation action for the *Regular Time Series* class:

```
/*
  PROGRAM          _RTAUTO
  DESCRIPTION      Producing of autocorrelation function plot of
                   an object of the Regular Time Series class
  USAGE            %_rtauto (object, element) ;
  PARAMETERS       object - the name of the statistical object of
                   the Regular Time Series class
                   element - the name of the column of the
                   statistical object
  REQUIRES         The &libwork is a global macro variable
                   defining the _SA_WORK library that contains
                   statistical objects
  AUTHORS          T.Kolosova and S.Berestizhevsky.
*/
  %macro _rtauto (object, element) ;

    %if %upcase(&object) = NULL %then
        %goto err_exit ;
    proc arima data = &libwork..&object ;
    identify var = &element ;
    run ;
    quit ;

    %err_exit :
  %mend ;
```

The implementations of the _ctauto() and _itauto() methods are available through the SAS Online Samples facility (for detailed information, refer to the inside back cover of the book).

You can use the following action

```
%action(object=travel, action="Autocorrelation",
params="air");
```

to obtain the autocorrelation function plots of the **travel** object that are presented in the output that follows.

```
                              ARIMA Procedure


                         Name of variable = AIR.

                     Mean of working series = 280.2986
                     Standard deviation    =  119.549
                     Number of observations =     144

                              Autocorrelations
```

Lag	Covariance	Correlation	-1 9 8 7 6 5 4 3 2 1 0 1 2 3 4 5 6 7 8 9 1
0	14291.973	1.00000	|********************|
1	13549.467	0.94805	+ |******************|
2	12513.692	0.87557	+ |*****************|
3	11529.066	0.80668	+ |****************|
4	10756.502	0.75263	+ |***************|
5	10201.181	0.71377	+ |**************|
6	9743.318	0.68173	+ |**************|
7	9474.212	0.66290	+ |*************|
8	9369.968	0.65561	+ |*************|
9	9589.176	0.67095	+ |*************|
10	10043.254	0.70272	+ |**************|
11	10622.369	0.74324	+ |***************|
12	10867.546	0.76040	+ |***************|
13	10185.330	0.71266	+ |**************|
14	9237.507	0.64634	+ |*************|
15	8374.002	0.58592	+ |***********| +
16	7688.441	0.53796	+ |**********| +
17	7142.378	0.49975	+ |*********| +
18	6699.134	0.46873	+ |*********| +
19	6429.540	0.44987	+ |********| +
20	6311.747	0.44163	+ |********| +
21	6534.630	0.45722	+ |*********| +
22	6895.620	0.48248	+ |*********| +
23	7390.765	0.51713	+ |**********| +
24	7606.043	0.53219	+ |**********| +

"+" marks two standard errors

You can conclude the following from this output:

- The autocorrelation function trails off very slowly, indicating month-to-month nonstationarity.

- There are spikes at lags 12 and 24, as you might expect with strongly seasonal data.

- The seasonal lags appear to decay at an exponential rate rather than at a linear rate, suggesting that the seasonal component is stationary.

The above results suggest that to remove the month-to-month nonstationarity the first differences are needed.

Difference Action

The Difference action produces autocorrelation function plots of differenced data for objects of time series classes. The Difference action has the following parameters:

element   names the object element

lperiod   defines left value of period of differencing

rperiod   defines right value of period of differencing

The definition of the Difference action in the ClassMet table looks like this:

ClassMet table

CLASS	ACTION	METHOD	ACTDESC
Regular Time Series	DIFFERENCE	_rtdiff()	Produces autocorrelation function plot of differenced data for an object of the Regular Time Series class
Calendar Time Series	DIFFERENCE	_ctdiff()	Produces autocorrelation function plot of differenced data for an object of the Calendar Time Series class
Irregular Time Series	DIFFERENCE	_itdiff()	Produces autocorrelation function plot of differenced data for an object of the Irregular Time Series class

The Difference action is also implemented with PROC ARIMA.

This is the code of the %_RTDIFF macro program that implements the Difference action for the *Regular Time Series* class:

```
/*
 PROGRAM          _RTDIFF
 DESCRIPTION      Producing autocorrelation function plot of
                  differenced data for an object of the Regular
                  Time Series class
 USAGE            %_rtdiff(object, element, lperiod, rperiod) ;
 PARAMETERS       object - the name of the statistical object of
                  the Regular Time Series class
                  element - the name of the column of the
                  statistical object
                  lperiod - the left value of differencing
                  interval
                  rperiod - the right value of differencing
                  interval
 REQUIRES         The &libwork is a global macro variable
                  defining the _SA_WORK library that contains
                  statistical objects
 AUTHORS          T.Kolosova and S.Berestizhevsky.
*/
    %macro _rtdiff (object, element, lperiod, rperiod) ;

        %if %upcase(&object) = NULL %then
            %goto err_exit ;
        proc arima data = &libwork..&object ;
        identify var = &element (&lperiod,&rperiod)  ;
        run ;
        quit ;

        %err_exit :
    %mend ;
```

The implementations of the _ctdiff() and _itdiff() methods are available through the SAS Online Samples facility (for detailed information, refer to the inside back cover of the book).

To obtain the plots presenting the autocorrelation function of differenced data, you can use the following action:

```
%action(object=travel, action="Difference", params =
"air,1, 12") ;
```

This action produces the following output:

ARIMA Procedure

Name of variable = AIR.

Period(s) of Differencing = 1,12.
Mean of working series = 0.183206
Standard deviation   = 12.3095
Number of observations =   131
NOTE: The first 13 observations were eliminated by differencing.

Autocorrelations

Lag	Covariance	Correlation	-1 9 8 7 6 5 4 3 2 1 0 1 2 3 4 5 6 7 8 9 1
0	151.524	1.00000	|*******************
1	-46.944257	-0.30981	******| +
2	14.448005	0.09535	| + ** +
3	-14.681265	-0.09689	| + ** +
4	-15.000093	-0.09900	| + ** +
5	9.243052	0.06100	| + * +
6	-0.043609	-0.00029	| + +
7	-8.501764	-0.05611	| + * +
8	-9.237759	-0.06097	| + * +
9	26.655581	0.17592	| + ***
10	-21.255578	-0.14028	| + *** +
11	10.566554	0.06974	| + * +
12	-20.254692	-0.13367	| + *** +
13	13.209419	0.08718	| + ** +
14	0.377976	0.00249	| + +
15	9.899368	0.06533	| + * +
16	-16.540607	-0.10916	| + ** +
17	-0.051148	-0.00034	| + +
18	6.671223	0.04403	| + * +
19	-17.265401	-0.11395	| + ** +
20	-13.829785	-0.09127	| + ** +
21	6.355321	0.04194	| + * +
22	-23.834143	-0.15730	| + *** +
23	39.033032	0.25760	| + ***
24	8.005913	0.05284	| + * +

"+" marks two standard errors

You can conclude the following from this output:

- The autocorrelation function presents a stationary process.

- The pattern of negative spikes at lags 1 and 12 with positive spikes at lags 2, 11, and 13 indicate a multiplicative seasonal model. The autocorrelations at all lags are 0, which is appropriate for the multiplicative model.

Action for Model Estimation and Diagnostic Statistics

In this section we consider an action that analyzes regularly spaced univariate time series with the ARIMA model.

For example, using this action, you can fit a multiplicative model, suggested by the interpretation of the autocorrelation function, to the international airline travel data.

ARIMA Action

The ARIMA action estimates parameters of the ARIMA model to fit a time series object of the *Regular Time Series* or *Calendar Time Series* classes.

The ARIMA action has the following parameters:

`element`   name of the object element that should be fitted

`model`   specification of a model to fit

`lperiod`   defines left value of period of differencing

`rperiod`   defines right value of period of differencing

The `element` parameter gets a single element of the time series object that should be fitted.

The `model` parameter defines which model should be estimated. The ARIMA action enables you to specify a wide range of models, such as autoregressive models, moving average models, mixed ARMA models, and factored models. We support SAS notation to define ARIMA models.

A model is defined as an optional specification of autoregressive and moving-average parts.

P specifies the autoregressive part of the model:

P=order or P=(lag,lag,...,lag)...(lag, lag,...,lag)

$P=(lag_1, lag_2,...,lag_k)$ defines a model with autoregressive parameters at the specified lags. P=order is equivalent to P=(1,2,...,order). A concatenation of parenthesized lists specifies a factored model.

Q specifies the moving-average part of the model:

Q=order or Q=(lag,lag,...,lag)...(lag, lag,...,lag)

$Q=(lag_1, lag_2,...,lag_k)$ defines a model with moving-average parameters at the specified lags. Q=order is equivalent to Q=(1,2,...,order).

The definition of the ARIMA action in the ClassMet table looks like this:

ClassMet table

CLASS	ACTION	METHOD	ACTDESC
Regular Time Series	ARIMA	_rtarm()	Estimates the ARIMA model for an object of the Regular Time Series class
Calendar Time Series	ARIMA	_ctarm()	Estimates the ARIMA model for an object of the Calendar Time Series class

Of course, the ARIMA action is implemented with PROC ARIMA.

This is the code of the %_RTARM macro program that implements the ARIMA action for the *Regular Time Series* class:

```
/*
  PROGRAM          _RTARM
  DESCRIPTION      Estimating of parameters of the ARIMA model to
                   fit time series object of the Regular Time
                   Series.
  USAGE            %_rtarm(object, element, model, lperiod,
                   rperiod) ;
  PARAMETERS       object - the name of the statistical object of
                   the Regular Time Series class
                   element - the name of the column of the
                   statistical object model -- is the
                   specification of model to fit
                   lperiod - the left value of differencing
                   interval
                   rperiod - the right value of differencing
                   interval
  REQUIRES         The &libwork is a global macro variable
                   defining the _SA_WORK library that contains
                   statistical objects
  AUTHORS          T.Kolosova and S.Berestizhevsky.
*/
  %macro _rtarm (object, element, model, lperiod,
                 rperiod) ;

      %if %upcase(&object) = NULL %then
          %goto err_exit ;
      %let model =  %substr(%bquote(&model),2,
                       %eval(%length(&model)-2)) ;
      proc arima data = &libwork..&object ;
      %if &lperiod = or &rperiod = %then %do ;
          identify var = &element ;
      %end ;
      %else %do ;
          identify var = &element (&lperiod,&rperiod)  ;
      %end ;
      e &model;
      run ;
      quit ;

      %err_exit :
  %mend ;
```

The implementation of the _ctarm() method is available through the SAS Online Samples facility (for detailed information, refer to the inside back cover of the book).

Estimating the parameters of a model for the **travel** time series can be done by submitting the following action:

```
%action(object=travel,  action="ARIMA",
params="air,'q=(1)(12)',1,12");
```

This action fits a seasonal moving-average model. The results of this macro are presented in the following output:

```
                    ARIMA Procedure

          Conditional Least Squares Estimation

                              Approx.
        Parameter  Estimate   Std Error  T Ratio  Lag
         MU         0.20666    0.63754    0.32    0
         MA1,1      0.31090    0.08461    3.67    1
         MA2,1      0.11364    0.10222    1.11    12

          Constant Estimate  = 0.20665715

          Variance  Estimate = 138.578707
          Std Error Estimate = 11.7719458
          AIC                = 1020.74545*
          SBC                = 1029.37104*
          Number of Residuals=       131
          * Does not include log determinant.

            Correlations of the Estimates

        Parameter     MU      MA1,1     MA2,1

         MU          1.000    0.014     0.033
         MA1,1       0.014    1.000    -0.050
         MA2,1       0.033   -0.050     1.000

           Autocorrelation Check of Residuals

To Lag  Chi Square  DF  Prob                    Autocorrelations
6       5.11        4   0.276   0.000   0.048  -0.104  -0.154   0.009  -0.023
12      11.12       10  0.349  -0.091  -0.065   0.125  -0.108   0.046  -0.017
18      15.02       16  0.523   0.078   0.048   0.019  -0.123  -0.039  -0.020
24      41.28       22  0.008  -0.178  -0.142  -0.024  -0.087   0.289   0.143


                 Model for variable AIR

              Estimated Mean = 0.20665715
            Period(s) of Differencing = 1,12.

                Moving Average Factors
               Factor 1: 1 - 0.3109 B**(1)
               Factor 2: 1 - 0.11364 B**(12)
```

Most of the Q statistics in the autocorrelation check of residuals are not significant, indicating that the model provides a good fit to the data; this model adequately describes the behavior of the international airline travel time series.

Summary

This chapter has shown how to create, visualize, and analyze time series in SAS, using an object-oriented approach to statistical programming and analysis.

Time series analysis was chosen as an example of a data analysis problem that could be solved using the proposed approach. The same approach can be used for solving other data analysis problems.

To summarize this chapter, let's analyze the process of solving a specific problem:

1. We started from a definition of statistical classes – in our example we defined time series classes. We specified characteristics that differentiate one statistical class from another. This definition is done only once, and can be performed either by the data analyst or by the data analyst together with a statistician. The data analyst then knows how to classify statistical objects.

2. The statistician specifies actions permitted for each statistical class. At this step, the statistician, who operates with strict definition of statistical classes, does not need to interact with the data analyst. The statistician does not need to specify all actions at once, because it is possible to add new actions as they are needed. The statistician, once acquainted with SAS capabilities, can define actions in SAS terms, thus making programming much easier and more straightforward.

3. As soon as at least one action is defined, the programmer can start implementing this action. Implementation of an action usually differs from class to class; however, the same action must have much in common for different implementations (otherwise, why use the same action?). This feature enables the programmer to widely reuse previously written code. Another peculiarity of object-oriented programming is that the programmer deals with statistical object definitions from the data dictionary, but not with the object itself. Thus, changes in statistical objects or data objects will never cause changes in programs. As a result, testing and maintenance of such software applications are easier and more reliable.

4. Finally, when some actions are implemented, the data analyst can start using them. Thanks to the object-oriented approach, all implementations are transparent for the data analyst. The data analyst only asks to apply the specific action to the statistical object. This approach guarantees the correct implementation of the required action.

Glossary

abstract superclass	a class that is only used as a superclass for other classes. In this case this class only specifies attributes, and subclasses must define the attributes of this class.
action	an operation that is defined for a class and can be executed by any object created from that class.
attribute	a characteristic that is associated with a statistical object. All objects of the same class have the same set of attributes. These attributes are specified by name, type, and initial value, and they are automatically initialized when an object is created.
class	the template or model for a statistical object, which includes data describing the object's characteristics (attributes) and actions that it can perform.
data object	data organized into coherent collections having specific structure.
foreign key	used to "link" related tables together. A foreign key is a column, or set of columns that defines a data value that must exist in some other related table as that other table's primary key.
generic action	an action that is common for a wide variety of classes.
generic macro	a macro that processes many different classes of objects and calls appropriate methods for each object that it processes.
implicit attribute	the attribute shared by all statistical objects.
index	a column that allows direct access to the rows in a table.
inheritance	the mechanism that allows a class One to inherit attributes and actions of class Two without the need to recreate/redefine them. The class One should supply only attributes and actions that need to be different from those inherited.
meaning	a way to replace an uninformative value with meaningful text. The definition of the meaning for a column is merely a reference to the table and its column that contains meaningful text. The column for which meaning is defined has to be a foreign key of the table that contains meaningful text.
method	the specific implementation of an action for a specific class.
object	a specific representation of a class.
primary key	a column, or set of columns, that makes each row of the table unique. Any column or columns can be used as the primary key as long as it defines a unique value for every row in the table.
statistical object	an object consisting of data with certain attributes.

subclass   a class that inherits from another class. For example, a class *One* is called a subclass of class *Two*, if class *One* inherits from class *Two*.

superclass   the class that another class inherits from. For example, a class *Two* is called superclass of class *One*, if class *One* inherits from class *Two*.

Index

Call your local SAS® office to order these other books and tapes available through the Books by Users℠ program:

An Array of Challenges — Test Your SAS® Skills
by **Robert Virgile**..................................Order No. A55625

Applied Multivariate Statistics with SAS® Software
by **Ravindra Khattree**
and **Dayanand N. Naik**........................Order No. A55234

Applied Statistics and the SAS® Programming Language, Fourth Edition
by **Ronald P. Cody**
and **Jeffrey K. Smith**...........................Order No. A55984

Beyond the Obvious with SAS® Screen Control Language
by **Don Stanley** ....Order No. A55073

Carpenter's Complete Guide to the SAS® Macro Language
by **Art Carpenter** ....Order No. A56100

The Cartoon Guide to Statistics
by **Larry Gonick**
and **Woollcott Smith**...........................Order No. A55153

Categorical Data Analysis Using the SAS® System
by **Maura E. Stokes, Charles E. Davis,**
and **Gary G. Koch** ....Order No. A55320

Common Statistical Methods for Clinical Research with SAS® Examples
by **Glenn A. Walker**..............................Order No. A55991

Concepts and Case Studies in Data Management
by **William S. Calvert**
and **J. Meimei Ma**................................Order No. A55220

Essential Client/Server Survival Guide, Second Edition
by **Robert Orfali, Dan Harkey,**
and **Jeri Edwards**................................Order No. A56285

Extending SAS® Survival Analysis Techniques for Medical Research
by **Alan Cantor**....................................Order No. A55504

A Handbook of Statistical Analysis using SAS
by **B.S. Everitt**
and **G. Der**...Order No. A56378

The How-To Book for SAS/GRAPH® Software
by **Thomas Miron** ....Order No. A55203

In the Know ... SAS® Tips and Techniques From Around the Globe
by **Phil Mason** ....Order No. A55513

Learning SAS® in the Computer Lab
by **Rebecca J. Elliott** ....Order No. A55273

The Little SAS® Book: A Primer
by **Lora D. Delwiche**
and **Susan J. Slaughter**.......................Order No. A55200

Mastering the SAS® System, Second Edition
by **Jay A. Jaffe** ....Order No. A55123

The Next Step: Integrating the Software Life Cycle with SAS® Programming
by **Paul Gill** ....Order No. A55697

Painless Windows 3.1: A Beginner's Handbook for SAS® Users
by **Jodie Gilmore** ....Order No. A55505

Painless Windows: A Handbook for SAS® Users
by **Jodie Gilmore** ....Order No. A55769

Professional SAS® Programming Secrets, Second Edition
by **Rick Aster**
and **Rhena Seidman** ....Order No. A56279

Professional SAS® User Interfaces
by **Rick Aster** ....Order No. A56197

Quick Results with SAS/GRAPH® Software
by **Arthur L. Carpenter**
and **Charles E. Shipp** ....Order No. A55127

Quick Start to Data Analysis with SAS®
by **Frank C. Dilorio**
and **Kenneth A. Hardy**.........................Order No. A55550

Reporting from the Field: SAS® Software Experts Present Real-World Report-Writing Applications ....Order No. A55135

SAS® Applications Programming: A Gentle Introduction
by **Frank C. Dilorio** ....Order No. A55193

SAS® Foundations: From Installation to Operation
by **Rick Aster** ....Order No. A55093

SAS® Programming by Example
by **Ron Cody**
and **Ray Pass** ....Order No. A55126

SAS® Programming for Researchers and Social Scientists
by **Paul E. Spector**..............................Order No. A56199

SAS® Software Roadmaps: Your Guide to Discovering the SAS® System
by **Laurie Burch**
and **SherriJoyce King** ....Order No. A56195

SAS® Software Solutions
by **Thomas Miron**.................................Order No. A56196

SAS® System for Elementary Statistical Analysis, Second Edition
by **Sandra D. Schlotzhauer**
and **Dr. Ramon C. Littell**......................Order No. A55172

SAS® System for Forecasting Time Series, 1986 Edition
by **John C. Brocklebank**
and **David A. Dickey** ....Order No. A5612

SAS® System for Linear Models, Third Edition
by **Ramon C. Littell, Rudolf J. Freund,**
and **Philip C. Spector** ....Order No. A56140

SAS® System for Mixed Models
by **Ramon C. Littell, George A. Milliken, Walter W. Stroup,**
and **Russell W. Wolfinger** ....Order No. A55235

SAS® System for Regression, Second Edition
by **Rudolf J. Freund**
and **Ramon C. Littell**...........................Order No. A56141

SAS® System for Statistical Graphics, First Edition
by **Michael Friendly** ....Order No. A56143

SAS® Today! A Year of Terrific Tips
by **Helen Carey**
and **Ginger Carey** ....Order No. A55662

The SAS® Workbook and Solutions (books in this set also sold separately)
by **Ron Cody** ....Order No. A55594

Selecting Statistical Techniques for Social Science Data: A Guide for SAS® Users
by **Laura Klem, Kathleen B. Welch,**
Terrence N. Davidson, Willard L. Rodgers,
and **Patrick M. O'Malley** ....Order No. A55854

Statistical Quality Control Using the SAS® System
by **Dennis W. King, Ph.D**.....................Order No. A55232

A Step-by-Step Approach to Using the SAS® System for Univariate and Multivariate Statistics
by **Larry Hatcher**
and **Edward Stepanski** ....Order No. A55072

Strategic Data Warehousing Principles Using SAS® Software
by **Peter R. Welbrock** ....Order No. A56278

Survival Analysis Using the SAS® System: A Practical Guide
by **Paul D. Allison** ....Order No. A55233

Table-Driven Strategies for Rapid SAS® Applications Development
by **Tanya Kolosova**
and **Samuel Berestizhevsky** ....Order No. A55198

Tuning SAS® Applications in the MVS Environment
by **Michael A. Raithel** ....Order No. A55231

Univariate and Multivariate General Linear Models: Theory and Applications Using SAS® Software
by **Neil H. Timm**
and **Tammy A. Mieczkowski** ....Order No. A55809

Working with the SAS® System
by **Erik W. Tilanus** ....Order No. A55190

Your Guide to Survey Research Using the SAS® System
by **Archer Gravely** ....Order No. A55688

Audio Tapes

100 Essential SAS® Software Concepts (set of two)
by **Rick Aster** ....Order No. A55309

A Look at SAS® Files (set of two)
by **Rick Aster** ....Order No. A55207

*Welcome * Bienvenue * Willkommen * Yohkoso * Bienvenido*

SAS® Publications Is Easy to Reach

Visit our SAS Publications Web page located at www.sas.com/pubs/

You will find product and service details, including

- **sample chapters**
- **tables of contents**
- **author biographies**
- **book reviews**

Learn about

- **regional user groups conferences**
- **trade show sites and dates**
- **authoring opportunities**
- **custom textbooks**
- **FREE Desk copies**

Order books with ease at our secured Web page!

Explore all the services that Publications has to offer!

Your Listserv Subscription Brings the News to You Automatically

Do you want to be among the first to learn about the latest books and services available from SAS Publications?
Subscribe to our listserv **newdocnews-l** and automatically receive the following once each month: a description
of the new titles, the applicable environments or operating systems, and the applicable SAS release(s). To subscribe:

1. Send an e-mail message to **listserv@vm.sas.com**

2. Leave the "Subject" line blank

3. Use the following text for your message:

   subscribe newdocnews-l *your-first-name your-last-name*

   For example: subscribe newdocnews-l John Doe

   Please note: newdocnews-l ◄——— that's the letter "l" not the number "1".

For customers outside the U.S., contact your local SAS office for listserv information.

Create Customized Textbooks Quickly, Easily, and Affordably

SelecText™ offers instructors at U.S. colleges and universities a way to create custom textbooks for courses that teach students how to use SAS software.

For more information, see our Web page at **www.sas.com/selectext/**, or contact our SelecText coordinators by sending e-mail to **selectext@sas.com**.

You're Invited to Publish with SAS Institute's User Publishing Program

If you enjoy writing about SAS software and how to use it, the User Publishing Program at SAS Institute Inc. offers a variety of publishing options. We are actively recruiting authors to publish books, articles, and sample code. Do you find the idea of writing a book or an article by yourself a little intimidating? Consider writing with a co-author. Keep in mind that you will receive complete editorial and publishing support, access to our users, technical advice and assistance, and competitive royalties. Please contact us for an author packet. E-mail us at **sasbbu@sas.com** or call 919-677-8000, then press 1-6479. See the SAS Publications Web page at **www.sas.com/pubs/** for complete information.

Read All about It in *Authorline*®!

Our User Publishing newsletter, *Authorline*, features author interviews, conference news, and informational updates and highlights from our User Publishing Program. Published quarterly, *Authorline* is available free of charge. To subscribe, send e-mail to **sasbbu@sas.com** or call 919-677-8000, then press 1-6479.

See *Observations*®, Our Online Technical Journal

Feature articles from *Observations*®: *The Technical Journal for SAS*® *Software Users* are now available online at **www.sas.com/obs/**. Take a look at what your fellow SAS software users and SAS Institute experts have to tell you. You may decide that you, too, have information to share. If you are interested in writing for *Observations*, send e-mail to **sasbbu@sas.com** or call 919-677-8000, then press 1-6479.

Book Discount Offered at SAS Public Training Courses!

When you attend one of our SAS Public Training Courses at any of our regional Training Centers in the U.S., you will receive a 15% discount on any book orders placed during the course. Each course has a list of recommended books to choose from, and the books are displayed for you to see. Take advantage of this offer at the next course you attend!

SAS Institute Inc.
SAS Campus Drive
Cary, NC 27513-2414
Fax 919-677-4444

E-mail: sasbook@sas.com
Web page: www.sas.com/pubs/
To order books, call Book Sales at **800-727-3228***
For other SAS Institute business, call **919-677-8000***

* **Note:** Customers outside the U.S. should contact their local SAS office.